THE POWER OF COVENANT IN TIMES OF CRISIS

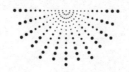

DR. RALPH PEIL
DR. SCOTT STRIPLING

To those suffering and dying from the worldwide crisis caused by the COVID-19 virus and those who perished on September 11, 2001.

WHAT LEADERS ARE SAYING ABOUT THE POWER OF COVENANT IN TIMES OF CRISIS

Each day, reports in the news serve as a constant reminder that we live in a complex and broken world full of escalating violence and turmoil. And yet, in the midst of this brokenness and violence, *The Power of Covenant in Times of Crisis* is a poignant and timely reminder that God is very much in control and at work in our world. Using a fascinating and unique combination of church history, insightful scriptural exegesis, biblical archaeology, and their own personal faith journeys, Dr. Scott Stripling and Dr. Ralph Peil remind us that as followers of Jesus, we can find encouragement, comfort, and hope in the very difficult and perplexing times that we live in.

– Paul Osteen, MD
Associate Pastor,
Lakewood Church

The Power of Covenant in Times of Crisis conveys clearly that while we may live in a troubled world, we are not without hope. The message comes through loudly and clearly that our loving God, who gives hope to all, has always been at work doing more behind our backs than in front of our faces. The reader will enjoy getting to know the authors and seeing many things from their combined experience and perspective.

– Ron Corzine
Founder,
Christian Fellowship International

We are living in days filled with chaos and punctuated with crisis as the post-modern and post-Christian West continues to unravel. Emotions are raw, and fear ubiquitous in this new age of self. Many of us look back to the events of 9/11 as the historical marker of this troubled new reality, but the current COVID-19 pandemic may prove to be equally significant. Enter *The Power of Covenant in Times of Crisis*, by Dr. Scott Stripling and Dr. Ralph Peil. This lucid yet penetrating new book is a reminder that it is God's covenantal promises that should drive away the darkness of despair and set us firmly on the strong and unmovable foundation of God's trustworthy character and word. The authors' creative approach brings the Scriptures powerfully into focus in a fascinating and informative way, reminding us of God's faithfulness in the past and calling us, as Christ's followers, to live Holy Spirit-empowered lives as God's covenant people!

– Scott Lanser
Executive Director,
Associates for Biblical Research

These two authors offer such a unique perspective of archaeology and love of biblical history – and an overall intense love of God – that, when using the backdrop of the infamous 9/11 attacks, they reveal insights and unique covenant implications that I had never weighed before! This book is a must for any truth-seeker who wants to delve further into God's covenant promises. The selected 9:11 passages point the way.

– Jill Mitchell O'Brien
President and Founder,
Kingdom Connections Int'l, Inc.

The Power of Covenant in Times of Crisis is a Texas-flavored spiritual fajita plate of delicious biblical exposition fresh off the grill, accompanied by a mix of tasty insights from ancient history and current events and topped with a zesty blend of unique life experiences of two men who know the inner workings of people and society far better than most through their somewhat unusual professions in medicine and archaeology. A good meal for anyone seeking nourishment in covenantal, transformational living that honors God and positively impacts society!

– Dr. K. Lynn Lewis
President,
The Bible Seminary

This book stirs the spirit of man to remember that God is active in our lives and encourages us to seek him and to move into what he is doing in our lives today.

– Walt Raske
Former Director,
Healing Rooms of West Houston

CONTENTS

FOREWORD

A physician who, like Dr. Luke in the New Testament, links his keen analytical skills with spiritual insight and a scholar-archaeologist who has intensely probed the soil of biblical lands join in this book to provide a fascinating view of the centerpiece of all history. God first gave his covenant to humanity in the Garden of Eden, recorded in Genesis 3:15. Medical doctor Ralph Peil and Scott Stripling, director of excavations at one of the most interesting ancient sites in the Middle East, show dramatically how God is intervening in human history to sustain and manifest his covenant. Using the attack on New York's Twin Towers on 9/11 and the COVID-19 crisis, they show God's fierce commitment to his covenant with the human race and how all of history's significant events point to it. Between every line of what many regard as "boring" history, covenant appears.

God takes the blood seriously. It is the very image of life itself, the river that carries the life the Creator breathed into Adam's nostrils in the beginning of humanity's trek across finite time and space. In God's intentional plan, the only time blood would be shed would be in the signifying of covenant. The cavalier shedding of blood that is so commonplace today is a mockery of covenant and the heart of the loving Father, who wants to be bound to humanity through Holy Blood – His own. That fallen state necessitated the Ultimate Bloodletting – the sacrifice of Calvary. First Corinthians 15:22 states, "In Adam all die, so in Christ all will be made alive." God worked all across history to establish the blood meme in the human psyche. Century upon century, the priests would offer up the sacrificial lamb so that we would be able to recognize the Sacrificial Lamb – the Messiah – when He came.

To put it another way, the Old Covenant is a trail of crumbs leading us to the Bread of Life.

The blood of the martyrs cries from the ground, and God remembers his covenant. Justice is coming. Deliverance is ahead. The crushing of the serpent's head is completed. The Kingdom comes. The Lamb is exalted to the Throne.

The blood reminds us, as Dietrich Bonhoeffer taught, that this victory of grace is no cheap thing. It is God's extravagant, extraordinary act to establish and honor covenant with his people.

Ralph and Scott show that those who read history through the lens of Scripture, with spiritual eyes, find amidst its tragedies great hope: God has not given up on his covenant... He has not abandoned humanity!

– Wallace Henley
Senior Associate Pastor,
Second Baptist Church of Houston,
Co-author, *God and Churchill*,
Columnist, *The Christian Post*

INTRODUCTION

Ralph Peil here. Scott and I have been friends for over twenty years. We've served together on a non-profit board, worked on archaeological projects in Jordan and Israel, and spent many hours discussing the troubling state of world affairs with the aim of understanding them from a biblical paradigm. This book is essentially a digest of those many conversations. Throughout the book, Scott and I will take turns giving our thoughts. Clearly, we are both writing from within the Evangelical Christian faith community and make no effort to be covert about our presuppositions. First and foremost, among these is the conviction that the God of the Bible has not changed and is actively at work in our world.

Between us, we have over 130 years of life experience, some of which we share in these pages, especially in chapters five and six. Our goal is not merely to demonstrate the dysfunction in the world (this is all too apparent), but to paint a bold and hopeful portrait of God's hand at work amid the current depravity.

~

Scott Stripling here. I am a professor, archaeologist, and ordained minister. I have long believed that covenant provides the key to understanding the world of the Bible and of today. My quest to understand the background of the biblical text led me to archaeology. Through careful excavation and research of biblical sites, I have discovered firsthand the critical background that informs my understanding of God's eternal message to humankind.

The single most important concept for understanding God is covenant. You might be asking, what is a covenant? We sometimes use the word in our everyday language, mostly in the context of real estate contracts. Sadly, few of us have a very clear grasp of what makes a covenant special. A covenant is not a contract. Contracts are "meetings of the mind," mutual agreements between equal parties. A covenant, on the other hand, is a stipulated agreement between a greater party and a lesser party. The greater party establishes the role that each will play; the lesser party accepts the terms, rejects the terms, or negotiates compromises. Once the covenant is enacted, its terms (positive and negative consequences) are enforced. The agreement is the instrument by which God's relationship with his creation is to be rightly perceived. Some covenants, like the Abrahamic Covenant, are unilateral, that is to say, unconditional upon man's obedience. Others are bilateral, like the Mosaic Covenant, and are conditional upon man's obedience.

Some human agreements in Scripture are also covenantal. For example, the relationship between David and Jonathan was a covenant. Another example is marriage. In biblical times, Jews did not date before marriage. Marriage was a legally binding agreement with far-reaching consequences. A father chose a husband for his daughter or a wife for his son. This usually involved consultation with and the consent of all parties involved. Next, a *ketubah* would be created. The *ketubah* was the covenant document that listed what the man vowed to do for his future wife. It also enumerated the father's stipulations, including the bride price. Once the terms were accepted, the couple entered the betrothal or preparation period, usually a few months. Finally, there would be a wedding, where witnesses would add their blessing and accountability to the union. The conjugal consummation would often result in the stained sheets that would be presented as evidence that a covenant had been "cut."

I am pleased to join my good friend Ralph in presenting this new look at covenant. We would like to thank Cheryl Peil Loveday and Caryl Moses Fonseca for their generous help in editing the manuscript. Any errors that remain are ours, not theirs. We are also grateful to Wallace Henley for graciously writing the Foreword and Dr. Paul Osteen for his endorsement and support. We are convinced that the message of covenant holds the key to individual salvation and cultural restoration.

It is not an accident that this book was released in the midst of the COVID-19 crisis. Without a doubt, much good can come from a fresh perspective on the 9:11 verses in the Bible, understanding forged through a past crisis that can guide us during a new one. We pray that this work impacts many lives and spurs dialogue on how to experience God's best, both personally and corporately in our society.

COVENANT PERSPECTIVE

THE GOD OF THE BIBLE IS CLEARLY A GOD OF covenant, but does he still see his interactions with humankind through the lens of covenant? Early in Church history, in the mid-second century, Marcion taught that the God of the New Testament was different from the God of the Old Testament.[1] This was a form of radical dualism that is now known as the Marcionite heresy. We, too, err in thinking that God deals differently with modern man than he did with the people of the Bible. Sound exegesis requires that we rigorously go "then and there" before making an application to life "here and now." Our archaeological excavations in the land of the Bible shed much light on the "then and there"; our common sense, enlightened by the Holy Spirit, basic exegetical principles, and life experiences, allows us to make accurate application "here and now."

English is the dominant language in the modern world. At times, however, it is inadequate to express certain concepts, such as that of an event that shifts the spiritual and geopolitical atmosphere, impacting the very cultural and spiritual environment. In Spanish, such a word does exist: *"hito."* In English, the closest equivalents are the words "harbinger" and "watershed." *Hito* moments significantly shift reality, and after they occur, things are never the same. The destruction of the Jerusalem temple by the Romans in August A.D. 70 is the quintessential example.

Figure 1.1 – The temple as it was in Jesus's day (courtesy of Leen Ritmeyer).

The economy and identity of Jews in Palestine in the first century were directly linked to the magnificent temple and its surrounding structures on the massive Temple Mount platform.[2] With the temple's destruction (predicted by Jesus in the Olivet Discourse), the sacrificial system ended, and biblical Judaism ceased to exist, superseded by rabbinic Judaism, which grew out of the decentralized pharisaical system. Rabbinic Judaism found its milieu at Sepphoris in western Galilee, just four miles north of Nazareth.

Figure 1.2 – First-century residential district at Sepphoris (photo by Scott Stripling).

A similar *hito* moment occurred on October 31, 1517, when an Augustinian monk named Martin Luther nailed his Ninety-Five Theses to the door of the Wittenberg Castle Church, setting in motion a reformation that would fundamentally reshape the world as it existed at that time. No longer would the medieval Church exert stifling control over the religious and political lives of Western civilization.[3] The year 2017 marked the five hundredth anniversary of this monumental turning point.

Figure 1.3 – Wittenberg Castle Church (photo by Cethegus, public domain).

One of the most significant *hito* events of the postmodern world occurred on 9/11/01. Those who are sixty years old and older can describe in detail what they were doing when President John F. Kennedy was assassinated. Their children remember 9/11 the same way. To Millennials, the hijacked planes that struck the Twin Towers were like the bullets that struck President Kennedy on the fateful day that his motorcade passed through Dealey Plaza in Dallas, Texas, on November 22, 1963.

Figure 1.4 – Twin Towers under attack (photo by Ken
Tannenbaum/Shutterstock.com).

No longer would the West be able to bury its head in the
proverbial sand after 9/11. A new Islamic caliphate was
proclaimed in the ancient Fertile Crescent. A Qur'an-driven
movement stepped out of the shadows on that fateful day and
now manifests itself in many ways: Taliban, Al Qaeda, Boko
Haram, Hamas, and ISIS/ISIL, just to name the better-known
groups. While the labels change, the movement's radical
commitment does not – a commitment to apply the teachings of
Mohammed to bring about the destruction of "uncommitted
Muslims" and non-Muslims, especially Jews and Christians.
Apparently, their sadistic actions are entirely consistent with the
teachings of their holy book, which contains 164 references to

jihad. While there are non-military aspects of jihad, its primary meaning is "holy war." The Byzantine Christians learned this all too well in 636 at the Battle of the Yarmuk (today's northern Jordan). We have visited this battlefield where the Christian forces, led by Emperor Heraclius, were defeated by the insurgent forces of Islam. Within one year, almost the entire land of the Bible came under Islamic control.

Figure 1.5 – Yarmuk Battlefield (photo by Todd Bolen/Bibleplaces.com).

The drive from Jerusalem to our archaeological excavations at Khirbet el-Maqatir (Khirbet means "surface ruins," as opposed to a "tell," which has a layered profile) and Tel Shiloh, in the heart of the Central Hill Country, happens very early each morning. The predawn regimen begins with breakfast at 4:15, bus departure at 4:59, and devotions at 5:05. Just as devotions end, we cross through the Hizme Junction checkpoint.[4] There is a small window of time just as the sun is rising over the massive Transjordan mountains during which the Twin Towers in the heart of Amman, Jordan, some forty miles away, are visible. Like the Petronas Towers in Kuala Lumpur, Malaysia, they stand as a tribute to the technological expertise of the modern world. It was for this very reason that the Twin Towers in New York were targeted on 9/11. The message was clear: a new and high-tech jihad was initiated, the ultimate goal of which is a worldwide caliphate governed by Sharia law.

THE BUSH AND OBAMA ADMINISTRATIONS

Both President George W. Bush, who was the American president at the time of the attacks, and President Barak Obama, who succeeded him, demonstrated a fundamental misunderstanding of the theology that drives radical Islam, or Islamism. President Bush repeatedly misquoted a key passage from the Qur'an, 5:32, leaving out the most damning words. Here is what the verse actually states:

If anyone slew a person **unless it be for murder or for spreading mischief in the land** [emphasis added] it would be as if he slew the whole world: and if any one saved a life, it would be as if he saved the life of the whole world.

President Bush always omitted the twelve bold words, apparently in a feckless attempt to differentiate between radical and moderate Muslims. It is likely that the forty-third president, no scholar of Islamic literature, was merely reading what his staff provided him, but at least he understood that America was at war with radical Islam.

Once President Obama took office in January 2009, he set out to, in his words, "fundamentally reshape America." Throughout his two terms in office, he never once uttered the words "Islamic extremists" or anything similar. On the contrary, he continually defended Islam, the religion of his father,[5] while never missing an opportunity to point out and exaggerate the failures of Christians. Inexplicably, the president used the occasion of the National Prayer Breakfast on February 5, 2015, to lecture the Christian leaders and laymen who were present about the excesses of the Crusades, a topic that has undergone the sterilization of historical revisionism and twenty-first-century political correctness.

None of this came as a surprise to those who had read his autobiographies, *Dreams of My Father* and *The Audacity of Hope*. In a *New York Times* interview on March 6, 2007, he stated that the Muslim call to prayer was "one of the prettiest sounds on Earth at sunset." On a more positive note, at a memorial service on July 12, 2016, for five slain officers in Dallas, Texas, President Obama appropriately appealed to Americans to "pray for a new heart." President Obama never understood that Islam is an existential threat to Western civilization. President Trump has not hesitated to accurately characterize the enemy, but he has also advocated more of a Laissez-Faire foreign policy. What will be the beliefs and priorities of the future residents of 1600 Pennsylvania Avenue?

The COVID-19 crisis presents a new crisis which will cost many thousands, perhaps millions, of lives and incalculable financial devastation. This devastation limits the ability of people of faith to invest their philanthropic resources to help alleviate the world's suffering. Such crises catch us by surprise, but they do not catch God by surprise.

HISTORICAL PERSPECTIVE

The word "bible" (Gr. biblos) means "library." Within this sacred library, there are many different genres: didactic, poetic, prosaic, apocalyptic, epistolary, and narrative. Much of the Bible is technically classified as narrative literature – it presents truth by telling stories. The first five books of the New Testament fall into this category. Narrative literature normally does not contain direct instruction about what is right and wrong; that is to say, it is not didactic. Rather, it shows people living their lives, making decisions, and dealing with positive or negative consequences of those decisions. In other words, it is experiential as opposed to propositional.

Genesis opens with the great cosmogony, or explanation for the origin of the universe and everything in it. This dramatic account is immediately followed by the story of Adam and Eve's deception by the serpent and their subsequent rejection of God's law. There was only one rule in Eden, and it was simple: "Do not eat from the tree of the knowledge of good and evil." When our progenitors broke this command, they set in motion a series of events that we are still caught up in today. Even the most optimistic people recognize that the world is chaotic. In 2015 and 2016, Paris and Brussels came under siege by radical Islamic terrorists. Parisian authorities mandated curfews for the first time since World War Two. Almost weekly, there is a terrorist plot somewhere in the world. Gaza terrorists regularly launch rockets on Israel. In 2019, thirty-two public schools in the United States experienced mass shootings. Christians in Africa face unprecedented martyrdom at the hands of radical muslims. And as we write, the world is in a virtual quarantine due to the pandemic spread of the COVID-19 virus. The crises engulfing the planet have, sadly, become the new normal.

AUGUSTINE OF HIPPO

In the fifth century, Augustine of Hippo wrote his famous treatises, *The City of God* and *Confessions*. These works had a profound impact on the world for hundreds of years. In fact, his views on warfare – pacifism, just war, and holy war – are still studied in America's military academies. In *City of God*, Augustine contrasts the corrupt city of the world with the glorious city of God (the Kingdom of God). Covenant is the legal instrument for the realization of this city/kingdom. Augustine's dichotomy remains all too apparent. His father was a pagan, but his mother, Monica, was a devout Christian. Augustine was perplexed by what he viewed as the Church's inability or unwillingness to answer difficult questions. He left

9

the faith, became a teacher of rhetoric, joined the Manichean cult, and lived an immoral lifestyle. When his destiny, through God's providence, took him to Milan, he wanted to critique the elevated rhetoric of Ambrose, the renowned bishop of that city. In Ambrose, Augustine found far more than he was expecting; he finally met his intellectual equivalent and much more. Ambrose was a man full of the Spirit of God. He spoke with confidence and authority, which mesmerized Augustine. Monica's prayers were hydrogen, and Ambrose's preaching was oxygen. These elements combined to form "living water," which brought Augustine back to life. His revenant came one afternoon as he sat in his garden, contemplating his own vileness. He heard what sounded like a child singing, "Tole lege, tole lege," which, in Latin, means, "Take up and read." Next to him was the Bible, open to Paul's Epistle to the Romans. His eyes fell on 13:13–14:

Let us behave decently, as in the daytime, not in orgies and drunkenness, not in sexual immorality and debauchery, not in dissension and jealousy. Rather, clothe yourselves with the Lord Jesus Christ, and do not think about how to gratify the desires of the sinful nature.

Augustine would later write, "No further would I read, nor did I need; for instantly, as the sentence ended – by a light as it were, security infused my heart – all the gloom of doubt vanished."

Watch out world, here comes Augustine. As Star Wars fans would say, "There was a shift in the balance of the force."

SPIRITUAL AWAKENINGS

The type of conversion that Augustine experienced changes the spiritual atmosphere and destiny of crumbling nations, and the nations, as we see them in 2020, certainly need awakening and reformation. Like Herman Melville's Bartleby, the masses are apathetic or powerless to affect meaningful change. All too often, they turn to power-hungry tyrants who make promises that they can never keep. When asked to get involved to make positive incremental changes, like the alienated scrivener, they "prefer not to." "Ah Bartleby, Ah humanity!"[6]

In Acts 3:19, Peter extends a tantalizing promise to his dysfunctional generation: "Repent, then, and turn to God, so that your sins may be wiped out, that times of refreshing may come from the Lord." Repentance precedes refreshment. This pattern presents itself throughout the Bible and history. Second Chronicles 7:14 makes it clear:

> If my people, who are called by my name, will humble themselves and pray and seek my face and turn from their wicked ways, then I will hear from heaven, and I will forgive their sin and will heal their land.

The ancient city of Jericho offers a candid comparison of the obstacles faced by contemporary believers. The people of Jericho were polytheistic pagans, which is to say they worshipped the many gods of the Canaanite pantheon. Chief among these deities was the moon god. They were a wealthy people with a heritage dating back to Neolithic times. Their heavily fortified enclave featured a double-wall system. There was a fifteen-foot-high stone revetment wall that served as a foundation for a massive mud-brick superstructure that rose an additional twenty feet. These walls were impenetrable, yet when the Israelites followed God's specific instructions, the walls crumbled. Archaeological excavations at Jericho in the 1930s by John Garstang and in the 1950s by Kathleen Kenyon confirmed how the walls fell. Garstang dated the collapse to about 1400 B.C., the time of the Israelite conquest, but Kenyon dated the collapse 150 years earlier. Although Kenyon was off on her dating, her drawings show exactly what happened.[7]

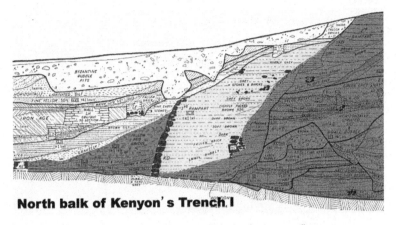

Figure 1.6 – Kenyon's drawing (courtesy of Bryant Wood).

The mud-brick superstructure collapsed outward, creating a perfect ramp for Joshua and his men to enter the city. What had been their greatest obstacle became the ramp to their destiny. Culturally, we find ourselves in a similar situation, with seemingly insurmountable obstacles of moral relativism, multi-culturalism, crushing debt, and weakened defense capabilities – just to name a few. However, if the Bible provides a blueprint for cultural success and renewal, and we believe that it does, these obstacles should actually be seen as opportunities that can form a ramp to our destiny.

DEPRAVITY AND HOPE

We offer this example. Due to the non-enforcement of U.S. immigration laws, approximately 5% of all people living in the U.S. are here illegally. This represents about sixteen million people from all over the world. Another 5%, most from non-Christian (largely Muslim) nations, have been "legally" processed into the country. The people in this 10% have a much higher birth rate than native inhabitants, and they have no interest in adopting the Judeo-Christian heritage and Protestant work ethic that made America the greatest nation of the modern era. This is the bad news. The good news is that we no longer have to go to the far reaches of the planet to do missionary work. The world has come to us. They live in our neighborhoods, attend our schools, and work alongside us.

While reform of the nation's immigration and welfare systems is a lofty and important goal, we should concern ourselves with the eternal destinies of the foreigners now in our land. How can we reach them for Christ? Whatever the strategy, it must be motivated by a deep and sacrificial love. First Corinthians 13:8 proclaims that "love never fails." Perhaps some of God's greatest victories will come at the expense of our foreign and domestic policy.

With biblical illiteracy at an all-time high, this will not be an easy task, nor should we expect it to be. An example of this was seen in a political roundtable discussion hosted by Anderson Cooper on CNN on January 12, 2016. One of the commentators waxed eloquent regarding her disdain for Ted Cruz, one of the leading candidates for the Republican nomination for president. Here are her exact comments (only stutters have been removed):

I don't know – this seems to have slipped through the cracks a little bit, but you know Ted Cruz said something that I found rather astonishing. He said, "It is time for the Body of Christ to rise up and support me." I don't know anyone who takes his or her religion seriously who would think that Jesus should rise from the grave and resurrect himself to serve Ted Cruz. I know so many people who were offended by that comment. [A fellow panelist inserts, "Wow," while the others nod their heads in agreement.] And you want to talk about grandiosity and messianic self-imagery; I think Ted Cruz makes Donald Trump look rather sort of like a gentle lamb.

It seems odd that a CNN commentator would make such a sophomoric mistake. It is extremely common in Christian parlance to refer to Christian believers as the Body of Christ (1 Corinthians 12:27; Romans 12:5; Ephesians 5:30). Even a casual exposure to Christianity would yield an awareness of this diction. Not only is the commentator unaware of this, but her colleagues appear equally ignorant. One can only imagine the outcry if the Qur'an were mischaracterized by a political hack. This panel actually believed that Ted Cruz, a committed evangelical Christian and the son of a pastor, was calling for a bodily resurrection of Jesus, who would then join forces with Cruz in a messianic (apocalyptic?) salvation of humankind. Cruz and all other Christians, of course, believe that Jesus bodily rose from the dead almost two thousand years ago, so how could he have possibly been calling for Christ's resurrection in 2016? This level of biblical illiteracy, combined with arrogant hubris, illustrates the depth of America's cultural divide.

Over fifty million abortions have been performed in America since the landmark 1973 Roe v. Wade decision. Abortion is one of the most perplexing issues of the modern world, but Christians have the certain promise that "where sin increased, grace abounded much more" (Romans 5:20). A few statements here will serve to illustrate the severity of the problems that stem from this diabolical industry. The depravity and greed of the abortion industry were laid bare before the world in 2015 when a series of videos were released of Planned Parenthood executives casually discussing the harvesting of body parts from pre-born babies. A simple YouTube search will reveal the practices of this cottage industry of death. The further along in the pregnancy, the more lucrative the market for the body parts. This necessitates support for third-trimester and partial-birth abortions. Millions of innocent human beings who would have survived outside the womb are being butchered in sterile clinics under the guise of women's health care. Half of the victims are females. What happened to those females' rights to choose? Shockingly, the people who exposed these horrific practices were charged by a grand jury, while the murderers and traffickers suffered no consequences. We contend that once a person kills his or her own children, his or her conscience is badly scarred and desensitized. Unlike Euripides's Medea, these people suffer far-reaching consequences.

HEROD'S MANIACAL MURDERS

A perfect example of this can be seen in the nativity narratives of the New Testament. Herod the Great ordered the slaughter of all male infants two and under in Bethlehem (Matthew 2:13–18). With a population of about three hundred people in the first century, this would have been about a dozen deaths. The reader may wonder how a person could give such an order. A little background elucidates how Herod became a maniacal megalomaniac.

As Herod aged, his paranoia grew. As an Idumean, he was never fully accepted by the Jewish population. To bolster his governing credentials, he married Mariamne, a Hasmonean princess. She was one of his ten wives. From 40 B.C. to 28 B.C., he murdered anyone in the Hasmonean lineage who could be perceived as a threat to his rule, including his "beloved" Mariamne in 29. In 7 B.C., he became convinced that Alexander and Aristobulus, his sons by Mariamne, were conspiring against him, so he did the unthinkable – he had them executed. They were strangled at Sebaste (Samaria of the OT) and buried at Alexandrium. Just days before his death, Herod had Antipater executed and buried without ceremony at Hyrcania.[8]

Figure 1.7 – Hyrcania Fortress (photo by Scott Stripling).

While we cannot know with certainty where Herod was when he gave the order to kill the Bethlehem babies, it is possible that he was at Herodium, the eventual site of his burial, just two miles away. In this scenario, from the high perch of Herodium, he would have seen and heard the slaughter in the distance. One wonders that if Americans were forced to see and hear the daily deaths at the hands of the abortion industry, they would allow this evil practice to continue.

Figure 1.8 – Herodium Palace/Fortress/Mausoleum (photo by Todd Bolen/Bibleplaces.com).

CULTURAL RENEWAL

Frankly, it is not enough to self-identify as a Christian. Cultural renewal will only occur as committed disciples bring the Kingdom of God to their communities. When full faith is placed in the finished work of Jesus Christ and not in his future return, believers engage the corrupt culture with great confidence in their ability to enact transformational change. In his famous "I Have a Dream" speech, Dr. Martin Luther King Jr. warned his listeners not to "take the tranquilizing drug of gradualism." Truer words have seldom been spoken. The time for change is now.

Bestselling author Leonard Sweet recently posted on Facebook the following:

The word "disciple" occurs 269 times in the New Testament. "Christian" three times, "leader" one time ("kubernesis" literally translates "captain of ship" [1 Cor. 12:28], which we translate as "leader" or "administrator"). The biggest problem of the church today? It's filled with "Christians" and "leaders," not "disciples."

We agree with Leonard. The timeless truths of the Bible have never been more relevant than they are today. Many of the biblical books with at least nine chapters deal with covenant-related themes; these are explored in chapters three and four. We are, of course, aware that the Bible was not divided into verses until the thirteenth century, and we are by no means suggesting some sort of "Bible code." Nevertheless, we find the 9:11 verses an excellent mnemonic device and a means by which the issue of covenant can be looked at with fresh eyes. It is the power of covenant that has sustained the Christian community over the last two millennia, and it is the power of covenant that provides the only hope of neutralizing the spread of Islam or of pandemic diseases such as COVID-19.

Much of the New Testament is the story of a terrorist with strong Syrian connections. Saul of Tarsus specifically targeted Christians, but after his dramatic conversion on the road to Damascus, he became a great apostle for the Christian faith. It is our sincere hope that many such terrorists in our time will also convert to the faith that they now persecute and exchange ISIS for ISSA. Issa (the Arabic name for Jesus) desires that each reader come into covenant with him – "Not wanting anyone to perish, but everyone to come to repentance" (2 Peter 3:9b).

In *Dreams and Visions: Is Jesus Awakening the Muslim World?* Tom Doyle documents hundreds of examples of Jesus appearing to Muslims in their dreams. Likewise, *A Wind in the House of Islam: How God Is Drawing Muslims around the World to Faith in Jesus Christ,* by David Garrison, documents this phenomenon. There are countless thousands of other examples from around the world. We have close friends (one a former student) who are leading multiple house churches in the West Bank of Israel/Palestine. Such things fly under the political and social radar, but they are having an important impact.

Regardless of the religious and political repression in places around the world, the truth is being revealed. Shakespeare wrote in *Julius Caesar* that "A coward dies a thousand times before his death, but the valiant taste of death but once." The future belongs to the brave and courageous. Carpe diem! It is time to once again embrace and advocate the timeless truths of covenant.

2

BIBLICAL COVENANTS

AN AWARENESS OF ANCIENT NEAR EASTERN CULTURE illuminates our understanding of biblical covenants. It is important to note that the Hebrew Bible (Old Testament) was written by Easterners and for Easterners. Since our readers are Westerners, it is necessary to illustrate the Eastern customs that guided how the Scriptures took shape. The writers used the literary devices and forms of the ancient Near East to communicate with their readers. In other words, the form and flow of the Old Testament are very similar to non-Israelite writings from the same part of the world at the same time. The book of Deuteronomy, for example, was written like a Late Bronze Age (1483–1173 B.C.) Hittite treaty. God is the suzerain, or sovereign, and the descendants of Jacob are the vassals.

COVENANT FORM AND FUNCTION

The basic form of the treaty or covenant is as follows:

- Preamble – The purpose of the agreement is established, and the identities and qualifications of the greater and lesser parties are introduced in the presence of witnesses.

- Prologue – The credibility of the greater party is illustrated through a recitation of his past faithfulness and generosity toward the lesser party and/or others.
- Provisions/Stipulations – The terms of the covenant are stated along with the rules by which the parties agree to govern their relationship.
- Payoff – The benefits of keeping the sacred oaths are enumerated, along with the consequences of violating the terms.

In his seminal work, *That You May Prosper*, Ray Sutton identifies five aspects of a biblical covenant. The acronym THEOS, the Greek word for God, can be used to remember these five points.

T – Transcendence: God is established as the sovereign. Who is in charge?
H – Hierarchy: Headship and delegated authority are stipulated. To whom do the parties report?
E – Ethics: Laws are enumerated. What are the governing rules?
O – Oath: God swears to bless those who keep the covenant and curse those who break it. What are the consequences of obedience and disobedience?
S – Succession: Inheritance and continuity are established. What is the future?

The Hebrew word that is translated as "covenant" in the Old Testament is "berith." This word is derived from a root meaning "to cut." The corresponding Greek word in the New Testament is "diatheke." Seven primary covenants drive the overall biblical narrative: the Edenic Covenant, Adamic Covenant, Noahic Covenant, Abrahamic Covenant, Mosaic Covenant, Davidic

Covenant, and New Covenant. Each one of these covenants has rules, the shedding of blood, and a symbol or seal.

EDENIC COVENANT

God placed Adam and Eve in a garden called Eden, located somewhere in Mesopotamia. The exact location of Eden remains unknown, but Genesis 2:10–15 describes the general boundaries. The Tigris and Euphrates rivers form the northern and southern limits. The locations of the Pison and Gihon rivers continue to elude researchers. Interestingly, the Gihon spring provided ancient Jerusalem with its critical water supply, and not surprisingly, an alternate rabbinic legend holds that creation happened near this spring.

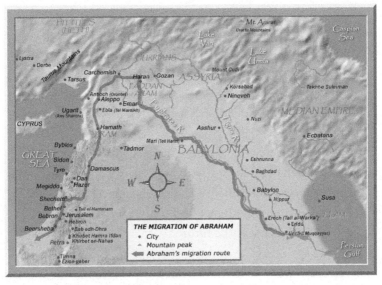

Figure 2.1 – Map of Ancient Mesopotamia (courtesy of Dr. David E. Graves, ECM).

In the Edenic Covenant, God assumed the role of the greater party, and thus he initiated the relationship. Adam, as the titular head of the human race, functioned as the lesser party. Two simple rules governed this first covenant. The first one was positive, and the second one was negative. God granted the progenitors authority to rule his entire creation, and he also gave them the privilege and responsibility of reproduction. Theologians refer to this as the dominion mandate.

God blessed them and said to them, "Be fruitful and increase in number; fill the earth and subdue it. Rule over the fish of the sea and the birds of the air and over every living creature that moves on the ground." Then God said, "I give you every seed-bearing plant on the face of the whole earth and every tree that has fruit with seed in it. They will be yours for food. And to all the beasts of the earth and all the birds of the air and all the creatures that move on the ground – everything that has the breath of life in it – I give every green plant for food. And it was so. (Genesis 1:28–30)

The next chapter of Genesis provides further details and a prohibition:

> And the Lord God commanded the man, "You are free to eat
> from any tree in the garden; but you must not eat from the tree
> of the knowledge of good and evil, for when you eat of it you
> will surely die. (2:16–17)

So, the rules were plainly stated. The covenant required that blood be shed. This occurred in the form of a tremendous blessing to Adam.

> So the Lord God caused the man to fall into a deep sleep; and
> while he was sleeping, he took one of the man's ribs and closed
> up the place with flesh. Then the Lord God made a woman from
> the rib he had taken out of the man, and he brought her to the
> man. (2:21–22)

Blood spilled when God surgically opened Adam's side. God thus became the first anesthesiologist and the first surgeon.

Interestingly, God planted a garden after he created Adam and before he brought forth Eve. First Corinthians 15:45 states, "The first man, Adam, became a living soul. The last Adam became a life-giving spirit." Eve represents the future Church, as she was brought forth from the side of Adam. Jesus, in his "sleep," was pierced in the side with a spear, and blood and water came forth. Eve was also brought forth before Adam fell into sin; likewise, the Church was birthed from the sinless life of Christ.

Adam's violation of the terms of the Edenic Covenant evoked strict consequences, including a loss of innocence and of fellowship with God. Adam was sentenced to a life of hard labor. Eve's punishment was twofold: pain in childbirth (including the entire female reproductive process) and submission to her husband.

ADAMIC COVENANT

With the ultimate goal of restoring the human race to an Edenic state, a redefined covenant was instituted. This is referred to as the Adamic Covenant. As a result of their lost innocence, the fallen couple made themselves clothes from fig leaves. From a covenantal standpoint, these textiles were wholly inadequate. This illustrates the futile attempt of humans to cover their own sins. Instead, God personally made them clothing from animal skins. Genesis 3:21 states, "The Lord God made garments of skin for Adam and his wife and clothed them." This sacrificial act reveals one of the great themes of the Bible – the shedding of innocent blood to cover the guilty.

It is impossible to know if Eve experienced a complete menstrual cycle before the fall. Regardless, this "bloodshed" after the fall was a regular reminder of paradise lost. The bloody birth of Cain would have certainly driven home this point. The dominion mandate remains in place, but now compliance occurs under the burdens of pain, parental frustration, subsistence challenges, and ultimately death. After the fall, they likely viewed death as both predator and prey. As a symbol/seal of this new covenant, a cherub with a flaming sword was stationed to the east of Eden, presumably to guard the tree of life (3:24).

The Adamic Covenant guaranteed a future redemption. Theologically, this is referred to as the protoevangelium, the first Gospel reference.

> And I will put enmity between you [serpent] and the woman [Eve], and between your offspring and hers; he will crush your head, and you will strike his heel. (3:15)

We will have more to say about this in the New Covenant section of this chapter. The Adamic Covenant is really the central focus of the Bible because it provides the pathway for postlapsarian (after the fall) humankind to reconnect with God. The subsequent covenants merely restate and expand upon the protoevangelium.

NOAHIC COVENANT

The descendants of Adam and Eve failed to obey the dominion mandate. As a result, wicked men dominated civilization in the ancient world. Their depravity was so great that God determined to destroy the inhabitants of the earth with a flood. Only Noah, his wife, their sons (Shem, Ham, and Japheth), and their sons' wives would be spared.[1] God instructed Noah to build a massive ark that would provide refuge for the eight members of this antediluvian (pre-flood) family, along with at least two (male and female) of each species of animal. Seven members of some species were quartered for the purpose of sacrifice and perhaps food. We presume that due to space constraints, the gathered animals were babies and that, like with Adam when his rib was extracted, God placed them into a state of sleep or hibernation.

This cataclysmic event required the institution of a new covenant. According to Genesis 6:18, "I will establish my covenant with you, and you will enter the ark – you and your sons and your wife and your sons' wives with you."

Although it had likely never rained (Genesis 2:5–6), Noah obeyed God. Once the deluge began, the rain continued for forty days and nights. It took 150 days for the waters to subside. Immediately upon disembarking, Noah sealed the covenant with blood. Genesis 8:20–22 states:

> Then Noah built an altar to the Lord and, taking some of all the clean animals and clean birds, he sacrificed burnt offerings on it. The Lord smelled the pleasing aroma and said in his heart:
>
> Never again will I curse the ground because of humans, even though every inclination of the human heart is evil from childhood. And never again will I destroy all living creatures, as I have done. As long as the earth endures, seedtime and harvest, cold and heat, summer and winter, day and night will never cease.

Figure 2.2 – Mount Ararat (photo by Steven Rudd).

The Noahic Covenant included two new legal stipulations. The first stipulation was dietary in nature (Genesis 9:1–5a). In the pre-flood environment, humans lived almost a thousand years while only eating a vegetarian diet. Many things were different in the post-flood world. Apparently, the canopy that created a perfect "greenhouse" for humans also filtered out ultraviolet rays that cause aging and skin-related diseases. With this canopy removed, lifespans plummeted to about what they are today. Noah's family and descendants were told to include meat in their diets. Among the reasons for this was the concept of sacrifice. Each time that an innocent animal was killed, humans were reminded that the atonement of their sins could only be accomplished by the shedding of blood. In this light, each meal was a covenantal celebration and reminder.

The second stipulation was civil. Genesis 9:5b–6 spells this out:

And from each man, too, I will demand an accounting for the life of his fellow man. Whoever sheds the blood of man, by man shall his blood be shed; for in the image of God has God made man.

Here God addresses the crime of murder. Murderers must receive the death penalty. Humans now have the heavy burden of determining guilt and applying capital punishment. In an earlier generation, Cain committed the first murder when, motivated by jealousy, he killed his brother Abel over the topic of sacrifice. In response, God uttered some of the most powerful and poignant prose in the Bible:

Listen! Your brother's blood cries out to me from the ground. (Genesis 4:10)

The Noahic Covenant placed murder at the top of the list of things that God hates. Later, the Mosaic Covenant would provide great specificity regarding a variety of capital crimes. Murder continues to plague humanity, and the blood of the innocent, including the pre-born, continues to call out to God. It is important to note that there is a difference between killing and murder. There are legitimate reasons to kill someone. Examples include self-defense, legitimate warfare, and capital punishment.

The rainbow serves as the symbol of the Noahic Covenant. This kaleidoscope of colors trumpets God's promise to never again destroy the earth by water (Genesis 9:11). The rainbow continues to mesmerize modern men and women.

Figure 2.3 – Rainbow over Jericho (photo by Scott Stripling).

ABRAHAMIC COVENANT

About four thousand years ago, God revealed himself to a polytheist in eastern Mesopotamia. That man's name was Abram, meaning "exalted father." Later, his name would be changed to Abraham, meaning "father of a multitude." Abram converted to monotheistic Yahwehism. Christianity, Judaism, and Islam all trace their faith heritage back to this patriarch.

Abram sojourned from Ur to Haran and from Haran to Canaan. God made covenantal promises to him at Shechem, and then Abram proceeded south to the hills between Bethel and Ai. After a trip to Egypt, he returned to this same spot, and it was there that he parted ways with his nephew Lot (Genesis 12–13).

There is little doubt that the location of the archaeological site of Khirbet el-Maqatir now marks this site. We worked together at this archaeological site, and Scott served as the director of excavations there from 2013 to 2017. A scarab found at Khirbet el-Maqatir in 2013 was voted by *Christianity Today* as the number one find in Israel for that year. It dates to the eighteenth Egyptian Dynasty (probably Amenhotep II), the period of the Exodus.

Next, Abram went to war to rescue Lot, and afterward he paid his tithe to Melchizedek, king of Salem (Jerusalem). Tithing was one of the stipulations of the Abrahamic Covenant, so it clearly predated the Mosaic covenant. Abram's military victory is an example of a legitimate war, or, to use the language of Augustine, a just war. This brings the reader to Genesis 15: the Abrahamic Covenant.

Figure 2.4 – Eighteenth Dynasty scarab from Khirbet el-Maqatir (photo by Michael Luddeni).

God initiated this covenant by appearing to Abram in a vision. As the greater party, the one who initiates, God establishes his sovereignty in verse 1:

Do not be afraid Abram.

I am your shield, your very great reward.

Abram, the lesser party, responds by acknowledging God's sovereignty and making his petition:

O, Sovereign Lord, what can you give me since I remain childless...

God responds by assuring Abram that his descendants will be as numerous as the stars in the sky. Genesis 15:6 powerfully affirms that "Abram believed God, and it was credited to him as righteousness." Abram was seventy-five years old at this time. The promise was not fulfilled until twenty-four years later. Along the way, Abram had doubts—all of us do—but he continued to trust in the covenantal faithfulness of God.

With the words of covenant having been exchanged, the next order of business was the shedding of blood. God instructed Abram to bring five sacrificial animals: heifer, goat, ram, dove, and pigeon. Abram knew exactly what to do with these animals, as this was how covenant was cut in the Intermediate Bronze Age (c. 2300–1900 B.C.). He split the animals in half, letting their blood pool in the middle. Like Adam, Abram fell into a deep sleep. God symbolically passed through the blood twice, once for himself and once for Abram. The first theophany was a smoking firepot, and the second manifestation was a blazing torch. This demonstrated God's awareness that Abram would never be able to fully keep the terms of the covenant. Fire is a common metaphor for God in the Bible. Two chapters later, God will give Abram the sign or seal of the covenant, which is circumcision. Again, the shedding of blood shows the seriousness of the covenant relationship.

Since the fulfillment of the covenantal promises of land and descendants was not conditional upon Abram keeping any terms, we refer to this as a unilateral covenant. By contrast, the Mosaic covenant was predicated upon the lesser party keeping the terms, so we refer to it as a bilateral covenant.

MOSAIC COVENANT

God told Abram that he would have many descendants; however, they would end up in slavery for an extended period. This is exactly what happened. Abram's grandson Jacob and his entire family found refuge in Egypt through his providential placement as the vizier (second in authority) of that country. Due to Joseph's exalted position, his family received favored treatment during the Twelfth Egyptian Dynasty, which was established by a group of foreign Semitic rulers from Canaan known as the Hyksos.

Once the native Egyptians expelled these Asiatic rulers, Abraham's descendants were forced into slavery in a xenophobic backlash. The Bible simply states, "Then a new king, to whom Joseph meant nothing, came to power in Egypt" (Exodus 1:8). There is much meaning behind this statement.

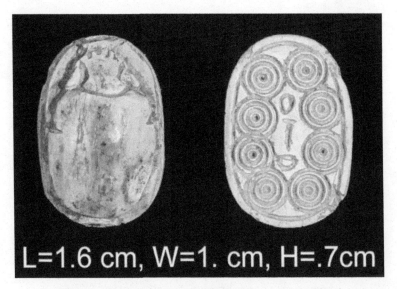

L=1.6 cm, W=1. cm, H=.7cm

Figure 2.5 – Hyksos scarab excavated at Khirbet el-Maqatir in 2014 (photo by Michael Luddeni).

In the mid-fifteenth century, during the Eighteenth Egyptian Dynasty, a deliverer named Moses emerged on the scene. In 1446 B.C., following ten devastating plagues, Moses led the Israelites out of Egypt.[2] Getting the Israelites out of Egypt proved less difficult than getting Egypt out of the Israelites. The Exodus became the pivotal and seminal event in the history of national Israel. The Israelites could not receive the law as long as they were in bondage. Once they were free, Moses led them to Mount Sinai to receive the law. There, God said to him:

> You yourselves have seen what I did to Egypt, and how I carried you on eagles' wings, and brought you to myself. Now, if you obey me fully and keep my covenant, then out of the nations you will be my treasured possession. Although the whole earth is mine; you will be for me a kingdom of priests and a holy nation. (Exodus 19:4–6)

It is important to note that the covenant promises that God gave were conditional: "If you will indeed obey my voice and keep my covenant, then you shall be my own possession."[3] There was more blood associated with the Mosaic Covenant than any of the others. An entire sacrificial system was put in place to atone for the sins of Israel. This is explained in great detail in the book of Leviticus. One verse summarizes the purpose of the entire sacrificial system. Leviticus 17:11 states, "For the life of a creature is in the blood, and I have given it to you to make atonement for yourselves on the altar; it is the blood that makes atonement for one's life." The blood made a way for each person to have a relationship with God. The Epistle of Hebrews speaks to the purpose of the Mosaic sacrificial system.

This is why even the first covenant [Mosaic Covenant] was not put into effect without blood. When Moses had proclaimed every command of the law to all the people, he took the blood of calves, together with water, scarlet wool and branches of hyssop, and sprinkled the scroll and all the people. He said, "This is the blood of the covenant, which God has commanded you to keep." In the same way, he sprinkled with the blood both the tabernacle and everything used in its ceremonies. In fact, the law requires that nearly everything be cleansed with blood, and without the shedding of blood there is no forgiveness. (9:18–22)

The entire sacrificial system served to foreshadow the coming sacrificial death of Israel's Messiah. The writer of Hebrews made the point crystal clear:

> The law is only a shadow of the good things that are coming – not the realities themselves. For this reason it can never, by the same sacrifices repeated endlessly year after year, make perfect those who draw near to worship. Otherwise, would they not have stopped being offered? For the worshipers would have been cleansed once for all and would no longer have felt guilty

for their sins. But those sacrifices are an annual reminder of sins. It is impossible for the blood of bulls and goats to take away sins. (10:1–4)

After completion of the initial conquest in c. 1399 B.C., Joshua erected the tabernacle at Shiloh, in the heart of the tribal territory of Ephraim, his own tribe. It remained there for over three centuries and served as the epicenter of Israel's cultic life. The Associates for Biblical Research (ABR), under the direction of Scott Stripling, opened a new excavation at Shiloh in May 2017. One of the research goals is to reexamine a massive bone deposit uncovered in the 1980s by archaeologist Israel Finkelstein.[4]

It appears that the only bones in the deposit correspond to the Mosaic sacrificial system. Strangely, Finkelstein failed to attribute this cultic evidence to the Israelites. The majority of the bones are from the right side of the animals, as prescribed in Leviticus 7:32. We are confident that the renewed excavation at Shiloh will harmonize with, not contradict, the biblical text.

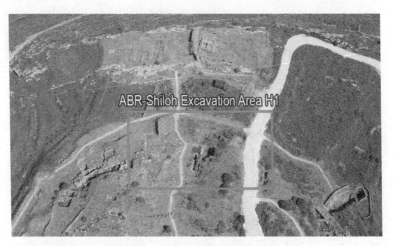

Figure 2.6 – Area of the ABR excavation at Shiloh (photo by Steven Rudd).

DAVIDIC COVENANT

Around 1000 B.C., God established a new covenant with David, the king of Israel.

The details of this covenant can be found in 2 Samuel 6–7. The blood of the Davidic covenant was shed when the Ark of the Covenant was moved from the house of Obed-Edom to David's tent on Mt. Zion.[5] First Samuel 6:13 states, "When those who were carrying the ark of the Lord had taken six steps, he (David) sacrificed a bull and a fattened calf." This continues the important motif of the shedding of innocent blood to cover the guilty. It is important to note that they could only go six steps, only a few seconds, without sacrifice. Six represents man's limitation, whereas seven represents God's perfection. David did not sacrifice every six steps, but only after the first six steps. Before the seventh step, there was an expression of humility. Man's sins offend God, and without atonement, fellowship is impossible.

David personally butchered the two animals while wearing the priestly linen ephod. Any hunter who has ever field-dressed a deer can vouch that it is not a pleasant process. David was probably covered with blood when he led Israel in jubilant celebration as the Ark was brought into Jerusalem. One thousand years later, one of David's descendants (Matthew 1:1) would also be covered with blood in Jerusalem. We will cover this in the next section.

God made two specific promises to David. The words of the prophet Nathan spell them out:

> The Lord declares to you that the Lord himself will establish a
> house for you: When your days are over and you rest with your
> fathers, I will raise up your offspring to succeed you, who will

come from your own body, and I will establish his kingdom. He is the one who will build a house for my Name, and I will establish the throne of his kingdom forever. I will be his father, and he will be my son. When he does wrong, I will punish him with the rod of men, with floggings inflicted by men. But my love will never be taken away from him, as I took it away from Saul, whom I removed before you. Your house and your kingdom will endure forever before me; your throne will be established forever. (2 Samuel 7:11b–16)

The two key promises in this passage are an heir and a kingdom. The initial fulfillment of these promises was found in David's son Solomon, but the ultimate fulfillment is in Jesus Christ. In the final chapter of the New Testament, Jesus states, "I am the Root and the Offspring of David" (Revelation 22:16b). In Peter's Pentecost sermon, he made it clear that Jesus assumed the throne of David when he rose from the dead (Acts 2:29–31). This is critically important.

The Davidic Covenant shows the loving kindness of God to all generations. This promise is stated in Psalm 89:2–4:

I will declare that your love stands firm forever, that you have established your faithfulness in heaven itself. You said, "I have made a covenant with my chosen one, I have sworn to David my servant, 'I will establish your line forever and make your throne firm through all generations.'" (NIV)

The Lord Jesus Christ fulfilled this promise and the promise of a new covenant – foretold by the prophet Jeremiah.

"The time is coming," declares the Lord, when I will make a new covenant with the house of Israel and with the house of Judah. It will not be like the covenant I made with their forefathers when I took them by the hand to lead them out of Egypt, because they broke my covenant, though I was a husband to them.... I will put my law in their minds and write it on their hearts. I will be their God, and they will be my people. (31:31–33)

In their genealogies, Matthew and Luke present Jesus as a son of David. In fact, the very first verse of the New Testament states, "This is the genealogy of Jesus the Messiah, the son of David, the son of Abraham" (Matthew 1:1). This verse inexorably links the Abrahamic and Davidic Covenants with the New Covenant. Frequently in the Gospel accounts, when people come to Jesus for healing, they address him as the "Son of David." Just before the triumphal entry, on the outskirts of Jericho, blind Bartimaeus is begging for money. Mark 10:47 states, "When he heard that it was Jesus of Nazareth, he began to shout, 'Jesus, Son of David, have mercy on me.'" The fifteenth-century martyr John Huss died singing these same words.[6]

Figure 2.7 – Area of Jericho in the first century (photo by Steven Rudd).

Jesus identifies Himself as the Son of David when he poses a question to the scribes in Mark 12:35–37:

How is it that the scribes say that the Christ is the son of David? "David himself said in the Holy Spirit, 'The Lord said to my Lord, Sit at My right hand, until I put thine enemies beneath thy feet." David himself calls Him 'Lord'; and so in what sense is he his Son?

Here, Jesus is quoting Psalm 110:1 and asserting that through his incarnation, he has become this promised Son of David. The apostle Paul also affirmed this in his introduction to the Romans:

Concerning His Son, who was born of a descendant of David according to the flesh, who was declared the Son of God with power by the resurrection from the dead according to the Spirit of holiness, Jesus Christ our Lord. (1:3–4)

Thus, when God said in the Psalms that he would establish his covenant with his servant David, a covenant of loving kindness that would be for all generations, that promise was fulfilled in and through Jesus Christ.

NEW COVENANT

The final covenant in the Bible is the New Covenant. About four hundred years after David, the prophet Jeremiah predicted the future creation of a new covenant. Jeremiah 31:31 states: "'The time is coming,' declares the Lord, 'when I will make a new covenant with the house of Israel and with the house of Judah.'" This prophecy found fulfillment in the spring of A.D. 33 when the long-awaited Messiah put this new covenant into effect through the shedding of his own blood.[7] Hebrews 9:15–17 makes this connection clear:

For this reason Christ is the mediator of a new covenant, that those who are called may receive the promised eternal inheritance – now that he has died as a ransom to set them free from the sins committed under the first covenant. In the case of a will, it is necessary to prove the death of the one who made it, because a will is in force only when somebody has died; it never takes effect while the one who made it is living.

Dozens of Old Testament prophecies foretell the coming of a messiah. The first messianic prophecy immediately followed the fall. God cursed the serpent and gave notice that humanity would ultimately be redeemed. Genesis 3:15, the protoevangelium, documents this first reference to a redeemer:

Cursed are you above all livestock and all of the wild animals! You will crawl on your belly and you will eat dust all the days of your life. And I will put enmity between you and the woman, and between your offspring and hers; he will crush your head, and you will strike his heel.

The Gospel writers give two names for the place of the crucifixion. The first is Golgotha, and the second is Calvary. The site was a stone quarry just outside Jerusalem's city wall in A.D. 33. Herod Agrippa I constructed a new wall in A.D. 44, which brought this quarry inside the city proper. This distinction is important because of the requirement of the Pentateuch that a sacrificial animal be slaughtered before the tent of meeting. Exodus 29:11 states: "And you shall slaughter the bull before the Lord at the doorway of the tent of meeting." The blood of the sacrifice was then taken by the high priest and sprinkled on and before the mercy seat. The flesh of the bull and its hide and refuse were burned outside the camp (Exodus 29:14). The sacrifice was not fully consumed until it was outside the camp, just as Jesus, as the ultimate sin offering, was fully consumed outside the gate or camp (Exodus 29:14 and Leviticus 16:27). The writer of Hebrews alluded to this requirement:

The high priest carries the blood of animals into the Most Holy Place as a sin offering, but the bodies are burned outside the camp. And so Jesus also suffered outside the city gate to make the people holy through his own blood. (13:11–12)

According to Matthew 27:33, the meaning of Golgotha is "place of the skull." Thus, Genesis 3:15 finds its fulfillment in the torture and execution of Jesus. When his cross was driven into Golgotha (the skull), the head of the serpent (Satan) was crushed. The Messiah's heel was only bruised. He triumphantly resurrected three days later. This became the core of the Christian Gospel. Every sermon in the book of Acts mentions the resurrection of Jesus. His resurrection reversed entropy and inaugurated the Kingdom of God. The extension and application of the New Covenant are synonymous with the Kingdom of God, a central focus in the teachings of Jesus.

For almost fifteen centuries, since the Israelites had first celebrated the Passover in Egypt, there had been an abiding hope in a coming Messiah. According to Isaiah 53 and Psalm 22, the Messiah would suffer a vicarious and atoning death to redeem humankind. Just before his betrayal and subsequent torture, Jesus celebrated the Passover with his twelve disciples. The synoptic Gospels all record this solemn event (Matthew 26:17–30; Mark 14:12–26; and Luke 22:7–20), and Paul wrote about it as well (1 Corinthians 11:23–25). About three decades after the New Covenant was enacted, Mark became the first to record the words spoken by Jesus that evening.

While they were eating, Jesus took bread, and when he had given thanks, he broke it and gave it to his disciples, saying, "Take it; this is my body." Then he took a cup, and when he had given thanks, he gave it to them, and they all drank from it. "This is my blood of the covenant, which is poured out for many," he said to them. "Truly I tell you, I will not drink again

---

from the fruit of the vine until that day when I drink it new in the kingdom of God." (26:26–29)

Jesus offered himself as the paschal sacrifice. Paul wrote of this watershed event in 1 Corinthians 5:7: "Get rid of the old yeast, so that you may be a new batch without yeast – as you really are. For Christ, our Passover lamb, has been sacrificed." This final covenant fully restored mankind to the conditions of the Edenic Covenant. Direct access to God was restored, and eternal life in heaven became guaranteed. Until Christ returns, the role of his followers is to fulfill the Great Commission of Matthew 28:18–20, which is really a restatement of the dominion mandate of Genesis 1:26–28.

Figure 2.8 – First-century stone vessel from Khirbet el-Maqatir (photo by Michael Luddeni).

GOD REMEMBERS HIS COVENANTS

So based on what we've just examined, it is very clear that God continues to deal with man through covenants. There is something else about that reality that adds incredible special meaning to it, something that should be a source of immense comfort to us all. It has to do with remembering.

It is a special thing to be able to remember. The mind is like a storehouse of treasures that can be accessed to review special occasions, such as weddings, graduations, and vacations. The capacity to remember allows people to think back on cherished memories. Neuroplasticity recognizes the capacity of the human brain to grow and reorganize based upon the thoughts one focuses on. In other words, focused memory and meditation upon God and his covenants help eliminate the negative thinking that too often consumes the human mind. The apostle Paul wrote about the importance of believers undergoing the transformational process of mind renewal: "Do not conform to the pattern of this world, but be transformed by the renewing of your mind. Then you will be able to test and approve what God's will is – his good, pleasing and perfect will" (Romans 12:2).

As amazing as the human brain is, God possesses a capacity far greater than the human ability to remember. Not surprisingly, "remember" and "covenant" are linked together fifteen times in the Bible. The first time is when God declares to Noah, "And I will remember My covenant, which is between me and you and every living creature of all flesh; and never again shall the water become a flood to destroy all flesh" (Genesis 9:15). Verse 16 continues: "When the bow is in the cloud, then I will look upon it, to remember the everlasting covenant between God and every living creature of all flesh that is on the earth."

The next time these two words are linked together is in Exodus 2:23–25:

> Now it came about in the course of those many days that the king of Egypt died. And the sons of Israel sighed because of the bondage, and they cried out; and their cry for help because of their bondage rose up to God. So God heard their groaning; and God remembered his covenant with Abraham, Isaac, and Jacob. And God saw the sons of Israel, and God took notice of them.

It was after this remembering of covenant promises that God appeared to Moses from out of the burning bush at Horeb, on the backside of the desert. This occurred when God called Moses to deliver his people out of their Egyptian bondage. After this occasion in the wilderness, an ongoing dialogue continued between God and Moses about how this deliverance was to be accomplished. God led Moses step by step through this whole process.

Moses's initial request to Pharaoh was as follows: "So now, please, let us go a three days' journey into the wilderness, that we may sacrifice to the Lord our God" (Exodus 3:18b). Pharaoh refused to grant his request and even made the Israelites' servitude harder by making them gather their own straw with which to make their bricks.

The Lord told Moses that it would only be under compulsion that Pharaoh would heed the request of Moses to "let my people go." The Lord continued:

> I am the Lord; and I appeared to Abraham, Isaac and Jacob, as God Almighty, but by my name, Lord, I did not make myself known to them. And I also established my covenant with them, to give them the land of Canaan, the land in which they sojourned. And furthermore I have heard the groaning of the sons of Israel, because the Egyptians are holding them in bondage; and I have remembered my covenant. (Exodus 6:2–5)

Even when God's people turned away from him in sin and rebellion, he promised that if they would confess their sin, if they would humble their hearts and turn back to him, "Then I will remember my covenant with Jacob, and I will remember my covenant with Isaac, and my covenant with Abraham as well, and I will remember the land" (Leviticus 26:42).

Prosperity is presented in Deuteronomy as a benefit of remembering the covenant. "But remember the Lord your God, for it is he who gives you the ability to produce wealth, and so confirms his covenant, which he swore to your ancestors, as it is today" (8:18). Covenantal faithfulness over time results in wealth. This is not to say that those in poverty are not in covenant with God (James 2:5), but rather that one of the indicators of covenant living is incremental prosperity (3 John 2).

God holds his people accountable to remember his covenant even as he promises to remember his. God said to King David: "But the loving kindness of the Lord is from everlasting to everlasting on those who fear him. And his righteousness to children's children, to those who keep his covenant, and who remember His precepts to do them" (Psalm 103:17–18).

Through the prophet Ezekiel, God promised to establish an everlasting covenant: "Nevertheless, I will remember My covenant with you in the days of your youth, and I will establish an everlasting covenant with you." This pattern of God remembering his covenant promises with his people in the Old Testament continues in the New Testament as well. When Zacharias presented his son John at his eighth-day circumcision, his tongue became loosed, and he uttered under the anointing of the Holy Spirit:

> Blessed be the Lord God of Israel, for he has visited us and accomplished redemption for his people, and has raised up a horn of salvation for us in the house of David his servant – as He spoke by the mouth of his holy prophets from of old – Salvation from our enemies, and from the hand of all who hate us; and to show mercy toward our fathers, and to remember his holy covenant, the oath which he swore to Abraham our father. (Luke 1:68–73)

Paul reminded his readers that at one time, they were alienated from God:

> Remember that you were once separated from Christ, excluded from the commonwealth of Israel and strangers to the covenants of promise, having no hope and without God in the world. But now in Christ Jesus you who were formally far off have been brought near by the blood of Christ. For He Himself is our peace." (Ephesians 2:12–14a)

Paul concluded:

> So then you are no longer strangers and aliens, but you are fellow citizens with the saints, and are of God's household, having been built upon the foundation of the apostles and prophets, Christ Jesus himself being the cornerstone, in whom the whole building, being fitted together is growing into a holy temple in the Lord; in whom you also are being built together into a dwelling of God in the Spirit. (Ephesians 2:19–22)

People cannot remember the day they were born physically, but followers of Christ and believers in the Gospel, should be able to remember the day they were born again spiritually. Believers may not remember the date, but they most likely remember where they were and the prayer that they prayed.

Jesus said, "Truly, truly, I say to you, unless one is born of water (natural birth) and the Spirit, he cannot enter the kingdom of God. That which is born of the flesh is flesh; and that which is born of the Spirit is spirit" (John 3:5–6). God is real. He desires to impact lives in a very real and powerful way. It is an amazing thing to enter into a covenant relationship with the God of Abraham, Isaac, and Jacob. He is only a prayer away. "And it shall be, that everyone who calls on the name of the Lord shall be saved" (Acts 2:21). Like Abraham, all believers can trust in the unfailing covenantal love (Hebrew – "chesed") of the God of the Bible.

The history of our archaeological site at Khirbet el-Maqatir begins with Abram (later Abraham) in Genesis 12:8: "From there he went on toward the hills east of Bethel and pitched his tent, with Bethel on the west and Ai on the east. There he built an altar to the Lord and called on the name of the Lord." Twenty-five hundred years later, in the late fourth century A.D., Byzantine Christians built a memorial church on the site. We excavated this ancient church from 2010–2016, and like Abram, we called on the name of the Lord. Through archaeology, we have learned that if we listen carefully, the stones still speak.

Figure 2.9 – Excavation of the church at Khirbet el-Maqatir (photo by Michael Luddeni).

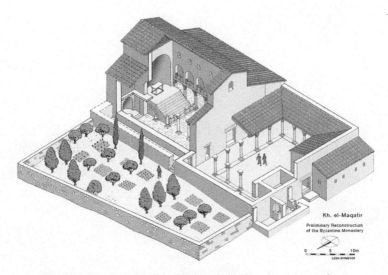

Figure 2.10 – Reconstruction of the church at Khirbet el-Maqatir (courtesy of Leen Ritmeyer).

3

SOMEONE CALL 9:11 - PART ONE:
THE OLD TESTAMENT

WHEN ISLAMIC JIHADISTS ATTACKED AMERICA ON 9/11, we never saw it coming, despite numerous warnings and a wave of internet chatter among America's jihadi enemies in the preceding days. God, however, was fully aware in advance, yet he still allowed it to occur. In simple but profound terms, nothing can happen without God's permission. Even more importantly, from Scripture, we know that if God allows an event, *it is for our ultimate good*, even unto death. Yes, good often grows out of tragic circumstances such as the 9/11 attack and the COVID-19 crisis.

This is Ralph speaking here. As I say that, you are probably even thinking of examples from your own life and experiences. The Apostle Paul's words ring true: "All things work together for the good of those who love God and are called according to his purpose" (Romans 8:28). I have been both a student and a teacher of the Bible for many years, ever since the Lord moved powerfully in my life when I was thirty-one. I am now seventy-eight. I was raised as an Evangelical, so not surprisingly, my approach to Bible study is serious and systematic. I have been blessed to sit under gifted teachers and preachers of the Word of God and have always tried to soak up as much as possible. Through my own study, I have always tried to independently confirm what was presented.

My wife, Charlotte, and I begin each day with a devotional look at the Word of God. In 2015, we used a month-and-day approach. For example, in September, we were reading the Psalms. On the first day of the month, we read Psalm 91, on the second day of the month, we read Psalm 92, and so on. On Friday, September 11, Charlotte had gone to run an errand, so continuing this study method on my own, I decided to expand my scope a little and read all of the eleventh verses of the ninth chapters in the Bible, the "9:11 verses." What I discovered, deeply moved and inspired me. It was the moment I resolved to write this book. Let me share the highlights in these next two chapters.

Christians believe that the Bible is the divinely inspired Word of God. Paul wrote to Timothy, "All Scripture is inspired by God and profitable for teaching, for reproof, for correction, for training in righteousness, that the man of God may be adequate, equipped for every good work" (2 Timothy 3:16–17). The writer of Hebrews echoed this thought: "For the word of God is living and active and sharper than any two-edged sword, and piercing as far as the division of soul and spirit, of both joints and marrow, and able to judge the thoughts and intentions of the heart" (4:12).

The Bible comes alive to anyone who possesses a serious intent to know the Word of God, regardless of how long he or she has been a follower of Christ. When studying Scripture, it is important to be aware of major themes and topics. It is also important to study Scripture in its context, with an awareness of each author's original audience and intent. However, the Holy

Spirit may illuminate a single verse or passage so that it becomes a rhema (living) word (a word for the moment). This applies to studying the 9:11 verses within the context of the entirety of Scripture, from Genesis to Revelation.

For the purposes of this book, seven books of the Old Testament were used. There are twenty-seven books in the Old Testament that have at least nine chapters and eleven verses. Seven New Testament passages were used. There are ten books in the New Testament with at least nine chapters. To maintain context, selected 9:11 verses are presented in the chapter and/or paragraph settings in which they are found.

GENESIS 9:11

And I establish My covenant with you; and all flesh shall never be cut off by the water of the flood, neither shall there again be a flood to destroy the earth.

The main word to focus on in this verse is "covenant." From Genesis through Revelation, God reveals Himself as the God of covenant. Genesis 9:1 begins, "And God blessed Noah and his sons and said to them, 'Be fruitful and multiply, and fill the earth.'" Next, God told Noah that he and his family were to "take dominion over the beasts or animals of the earth, over every bird, every creeping thing and all the fish of the sea." This is also what God said in Genesis 1:26–28 (the dominion mandate).

In essence, God confirmed to Noah and his sons what he had initially said to Adam. When Noah is first introduced in Genesis 6:5, the reader learns that "the wickedness of man was great on the earth and God saw that the thoughts and intents of man's heart was on evil continually." Genesis 6:6–8 states, "And the

Lord was sorry that He had made man on the earth, and he was grieved in His heart… But Noah found favor in the eyes of the Lord."

After the Lord spoke to Noah (v. 13), he instructed him to build the ark according to detailed specifications: 450 feet in length, seventy-five feet in width, and forty-five feet in height. It was also to have a window at the top and a door in the side. It was to have a lower, second, and third deck. In addition to Noah and his family, a male and female animal of each species would occupy the ark. The Lord then explained that he was going to bring a flood upon the earth that would destroy every living thing. God, however, established his covenant whereby Noah, his family, and the animals would remain safe during the flood.

One of the basic principles of Bible study is called the "rule of first mention." This means that in studying any topic or subject in the Bible, one goes back to where that subject is first used and then follows that theme through the Bible. This requires a reliable translation of the Scriptures, a good concordance or Bible software program, and some time and effort. This is a good way to study the Bible because it helps everything "fall into place" as a unified whole. With this approach, it becomes clear that the biblical narrative is consistent from Genesis through Revelation.

The first place that the word "covenant" is used in the Bible is in the story of Noah. As noted in Chapter Two, the covenant theme can be followed throughout the Bible. Importantly, it was God who established covenants. Repeatedly, he said, "This is My Covenant." He set the rules and regulations for how his people would live under his covenant promises.

This is where the study of the 9:11 Scriptures begins, with God establishing his covenant with Noah. "And I establish my covenant with you; and all flesh shall never be cut off by the water of the flood, neither shall there again be a flood to destroy the earth."

EXODUS 9:11

And the magicians could not stand before Moses because of the boils, for the boils were on the magicians as well as on all the Egyptians.

This verse refers to one of the ten plagues God brought upon the Egyptians, which Moses announced to Pharaoh so that Pharaoh would free the Hebrews from slavery. Exodus 9:1 begins with a description of the fifth plague: "Then the Lord said to Moses, 'Go to Pharaoh and speak to him, 'Thus says the Lord, the God of the Hebrews, Let My people go, that they may serve Me.'" These were the plagues that God pronounced as judgments against Pharaoh and the gods of Egypt:

PLAGUE	STORY REFERENCE	EGYPTIAN DEITY AFFECTED
Nile turns to blood	Exodus 7:14–25	Osiris (Nile was his bloodstream)
Frogs cover the land	Exodus 8:1–15	Heqt (frog god of resurrection)
Gnat/mosquito infestation	Exodus 8:16–19	Unknown
Fly infestation	Exodus 8:20–32	Unknown
Egyptian cattle die	Exodus 9:1–7	Apis (bull god – symbol of virility)
Boils	Exodus 9:8–12	Imhotep (god of medicine)
Hail	Exodus 9:18–35	Isis (goddess of life)
Locust infestation	Exodus 10:1–20	Seth (protector of crops)
Darkness for three days	Exodus 10:21–29	Re/Ra (sun god)
Death of the firstborn	Exodus 11:1–10	Pharaoh (worshipped as a god)

Figure 3.1 – Gods of Egypt (courtesy of Scott Stripling).

When God gave Moses the instructions for observing the Passover, he told each family to take a one-year-old lamb into their homes on the tenth day of the first month, called Nissan.

They were to care for the lamb for four days and then slay it on the evening of the fourteenth day. They were to take some of the blood and put it on the lintel and doorposts of each Hebrew home. They were told to roast the lamb and to eat it with unleavened bread and bitter herbs. They were also told to "eat it with your loins girded and sandals on your feet, and your staff in your hand; and you shall eat it in haste – it is the Lord's Passover" (Exodus 12: 1–13).

Yahweh then told Moses that he, the monotheistic God of the Israelites, would go through the land of Egypt on that night and strike down, or kill, all the first-born in the land of Egypt, both man and beast. God was going to execute judgments against the pantheon of Egyptian gods (see Figure 3.1).

The blood of the lamb on each house would be a sign. God said, "When I see the blood, I will pass over you, and no plague will befall you to destroy you when I strike the land of Egypt" (Exodus 12:13b). This was to become a day of memorial, and they were instructed to celebrate it as a feast to the Lord throughout all generations. They were also given instructions for observing the feast of unleavened bread. The sacrifice of the paschal lamb is still practiced each spring by the Samaritans on Mount Gerizim.

Figure 3.2 – Samaritan sacrifices on Mt. Gerizim (Photo by Todd Bolen/Bibleplaces.com).

This theme of the Passover lamb was fulfilled in the life of Jesus Christ. He began his public ministry after his baptism. When John the Baptist saw him coming, he proclaimed, "Behold, the lamb of God, who takes away the sin of the world!" (John 1:29b). In Isaiah 53, the suffering servant passage, the prophet Isaiah says that one would come who would be "despised and rejected of men, a man of sorrows and acquainted with grief" (v. 3), one who would bear sins and carry sorrows. Isaiah 53:6–7 states,

> All we like sheep have gone astray. Each of us has turned to his own way; but the Lord has caused the iniquity of us all to fall upon him. He was oppressed and he was afflicted, yet he did not open his mouth; like a lamb that is led to slaughter, and like a sheep that is silent before its shearers, so he did not open His mouth.

Jewish males typically traveled to Jerusalem one to three times a year to keep the various feasts of the Lord. Those occasions were the Feast of Unleavened Bread, also called Passover, the Feast of Weeks, also called the Feast of Pentecost, and the Feast of Booths or Tabernacles (Deuteronomy 16:16). Luke 2:41 provides a glimpse into Jesus's childhood: "And His parents used to go to Jerusalem every year at the Feast of the Passover." When Jesus was twelve, he went to observe the feast with them. After observing the full number of days, he stayed behind in Jerusalem, but his parents were unaware of this. When they missed him about a day later, they returned to Jerusalem to find him. After a three-day search, "they found Him in the temple, sitting in the midst of teachers, both listening to them and asking them questions. And all who heard him were amazed at his understanding and his answers" (vv. 46–47). When they found Jesus, he said to them, "Why is it that you were looking for Me? Did you not know that I had to be in My Father's house (or about the affairs of My Father)?" (v. 49).

When the time came for Jesus to become the ultimate Passover lamb of God, he instructed his disciples to secure a venue for the Pascal celebration: "The Teacher says, My time is at hand; I am to keep the Passover at your house with My disciples" (Matthew 26:18b). The apostle Paul told the Corinthians in 1 Corinthians 5:7, "Clean out the old leaven, that you may be a new lump, just as you are in fact unleavened. For Christ, our Passover also has been sacrificed."

First Peter 1:18–19 instructs that we have not been redeemed with perishable things, but with precious blood as of a lamb unblemished and spotless, the blood of Christ.

Even as Mary and Joseph searched for Jesus when he was in the temple, those who find him today must also search for him. The same could be said for the Magi of the nativity narratives. Isaiah 55:6 states:

> Seek the Lord while he may be found, call upon him while He is near. Let the wicked forsake his way, and the unrighteous man his thoughts; and let him return to the Lord; he will have compassion on him; and to our God, for he will abundantly pardon.

Exodus 9:11 speaks of the judgments God brought against Pharaoh and the gods of Egypt that freed the Israelites from slavery: "And the magicians could not stand before Moses because of the boils, for the boils were on the magicians as well as on all the Egyptians." The judgments culminated in the death of all firstborn except those whose homes were protected by the blood of the lamb on their doorposts. This ultimately points to Jesus Christ.

LEVITICUS 9:11

*The flesh and the skin, however, he burned with fire
outside the camp.*

What is this all about? The name for Leviticus comes from the pre-Christian Greek translation of the Old Testament, the Septuagint, and means "relating to the Levites." The Hebrew title for the book comes from the first word of the Hebrew text, meaning "and he called." God was again speaking to the sons of Israel through Moses. Here, God was speaking from the tent of meeting, which had been built in the wilderness according to the plans he had previously given to Moses on the holy mountain. God also provided Moses a list of sacrifices and offerings for the priests (Levites, primarily Aaron and his sons) to conduct. These sacrifices and offerings were atonements for their sins, allowing them to maintain right standing before God.

Figure 3.3 – The Tabernacle. (Photo by Bill Shlegel/Bibleplaces.com).

Two key verses that are given in Leviticus are 17:11 and 20:7–8. Verse 17:11 states, "For the life of the flesh is in the blood, and I have given it to you on the altar to make atonement for your souls; for it is the blood by reason of the life that makes atonement." Leviticus 20:7–8 declares, "Ye shall consecrate yourselves therefore and be holy, for I am the Lord your God, and you shall keep my statutes and practice them; for I am the Lord who sanctifies you."

The book of Leviticus also describes five main offerings that the people were to bring unto the Lord. They were:

1. The burnt offering – chapter 1
2. The grain offering – chapter 2

3. The fellowship offering – chapter 3
4. The sin offering – chapter 4:1–5:13
5. The guilt offering – chapter 5:14–6:7

Leviticus chapters 8–10 describe Aaron and his sons being consecrated as priests before the Lord and the congregation. They were first washed with water, given special garments to wear, anointed with oil, and consecrated with blood. After their ordination, they were instructed to remain in the tent of meeting (Hebrew – "ohel moed") for seven days.

Chapter 9 begins with Aaron and his sons coming out of the tent of meeting. Aaron is instructed to begin offering sacrifices for himself and for the people. God's purpose for the sacrifices was atonement for people's sins. In 9:6, Moses says, "This is the thing which the Lord has commanded you to do, that the glory of the Lord may appear to you." Importantly, after the sacrifices were made in the prescribed manner, the flesh and the skin were to be burned outside the camp (v. 11).

The glory of God appeared to the people in the holy mountain and also when the tabernacle (Hebrew – mishkan) was completed, as recorded in Exodus 40:34–38. This was the same glory that led the Israelites in all of their wilderness wanderings as a cloud by day and a pillar of fire at night.

In the New Testament, this glory was revealed in the Son of God when he became flesh. John 1:14 states: "And the Word became flesh and dwelt ("tabernacled") among us, and we beheld his glory, glory as the only begotten from the Father, full of grace and truth." This glory of God was fully manifested in Christ on the Mount of Transfiguration (Matthew 17:1–13, Mark 9:2–13, Luke 9:28–36). Peter also spoke of this glory of God being manifested in Christ:

For we did not follow cleverly devised tales when we made known to you the power and coming of our Lord Jesus Christ, but we were eyewitnesses of his majesty. For when he received honor and glory from God the Father, such an utterance as this was made to him by the Majestic Glory, "This is My beloved Son with whom I am well pleased," and we ourselves heard this utterance made from heaven when we were with him on the holy mountain. (2 Peter 1:16–18)

The writer of Hebrews proclaimed Jesus as the ultimate high priest:

Since then we have a great high priest who has passed through the heavens, Jesus the Son of God, let us hold fast our confession. For we do not have a high priest who cannot sympathize with our weaknesses, but one who has been tempted in all things as we are, yet without sin. Let us therefore draw near with confidence to the throne of grace, that we may receive mercy and may find grace to help in time of need. (4:14–16)

When Jesus died on a cross, he fulfilled all the sin offerings required by God in the Old Testament. Second Corinthians 5:21 states, "For He made Him who knew no sin to be sin on our behalf that we might become the righteousness of God in Him." When Jesus took the sins of mankind upon himself on the cross, he established a new covenant of grace for all mankind. He fulfilled all of the old and new covenant promises. God did this out of his heart of love for all people, for all time, so that all who call upon the name of the Lord might be saved. John 3:16 became a reality: "For God so loved the world that he gave his only begotten Son, that whoever believes in him should not perish, but have eternal life."

"The flesh and the skin, however, he burned with fire outside the camp." This was also fulfilled in the death of Christ. Hebrews 13:8–15 explains:

Jesus Christ is the same yesterday and today, yes and forever. Do not be carried away by varied and strange teachings for it is good for the heart to be strengthened by grace, not by foods, through which those who were thus occupied were not benefited. We have an altar, from which those who serve the tabernacle have no right to eat. For the bodies of those animals whose blood is brought onto the holy place by the high priest as an offering for sin, are burned outside the camp. Therefore, Jesus also, that He might sanctify the people through His own blood, suffered outside the gate. Hence, let us go out to Him outside the camp, bearing his reproach. For here we do not have a lasting city, but we are seeking the city, which is to come. Through him then, let us continually offer up a sacrifice of praise to God, that is, the fruit of our lips that give thanks to His name.

NUMBERS 9:11

In the second month on the fourteenth day at twilight they shall observe it; they shall eat it with unleavened bread and bitter herbs.

The book of Numbers deals with the wilderness wanderings of the people of Israel after they had been miraculously delivered from slavery in the land of Egypt. Their sojourn in the wilderness lasted forty years.

Chapter 9 describes how the Lord spoke to Moses, saying that in the first month of the second year after coming out of the land of Egypt, they should observe the Feast of Passover at the appointed time. The people did as the Lord instructed.

The Lord provided specific instructions to Moses and Aaron about who could observe Passover and how it was to be celebrated. Those regulations are recorded in Exodus 12:43–49:

1. No foreigner was to eat of the feast. (There were exceptions.)
2. A slave could eat of it after he was circumcised.
3. A temporary worker or a hired worker could not eat of it.
4. It had to be eaten inside the house.
5. None of the meat could be taken outside.
6. None of the bones were to be broken.
7. The whole community of Israel had to celebrate the meal.
8. An alien living among the Israelites who wanted to celebrate Passover had to have all the males in his household circumcised.
9. No uncircumcised male could eat of the Passover.

All of these regulations were part of keeping the covenant. There were some men in the camp (Numbers 9) who were ceremonially unclean because they had touched the body of a dead person. For this reason, they were excluded from observing Passover. When they asked Moses what they were to do, he asked the Lord, and the Lord answered him:

Speak to the sons of Israel, saying "If anyone of you or of your generations becomes unclean because of a dead person, or is on a distant journey, he may however, observe the Passover of the Lord. In the second month on the fourteenth day at twilight, they shall observe it; they shall eat it with unleavened bread and bitter herbs. They shall leave none of it till morning, nor break a bone of it; according to all the statute of the Passover they shall observe it. But the man who is clean and not on a journey, and yet neglects to observe the Passover, that person shall then be cut off from his people, for he did not present the offering of the Lord at its appointed time. That man shall bear his sin." (9:10–13)

This would be the last time the Passover would be observed in the wilderness. It would not be observed again until the sons of Israel had crossed over the Jordan into the Promised Land, camping at Gilgal, as recorded in Joshua 5:10–12.[1]

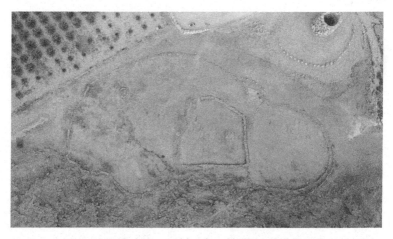

Figure 3.4 – Gilgal Argaman (photo by Todd Bolen/Bibleplaces.com).

Many significant events that happened to the children of Israel during their wilderness wandering serve as examples to believers and find ultimate fulfillment in the life of Jesus Christ. Five of those examples are the manna, the cloud and the rock, water from the rock, the fiery serpents, and the Passover.

BREAD FROM HEAVEN

God fed the Israelites after they complained to Moses that they had no bread to eat as they had in Egypt. The Lord said to Moses: "Behold, I will rain bread from heaven for you; and the people shall go out and gather a day's portion every day, that I may test them, whether or not they will walk in My instruction" (Exodus 16:4). They were instructed to gather twice as much on the sixth day so they could rest on the Sabbath. The bread was called manna, which literally means "What is it?" Moses told the people that the bread is illustrative of God's glory (v. 7). The provision of manna ceased on the day the Israelites entered the Promised Land (Joshua 5:12).

Jesus referred to himself as a representation of the true bread from heaven. John 6 tells the story of the feeding of the five thousand when the "Passover was at hand" (v. 4). Jesus asked Philip, "Where are we to buy bread that these may eat?" (v. 5) Philip said that they did not have enough money to buy bread for everyone, but Andrew spoke up and proclaimed, "There is a lad here who has five barley loaves and two fish; but what are these for so many people?" (John 6:9) After the people were fed, there were twelve baskets of food left over. Some of the people came seeking Jesus after he crossed the Sea of Galilee and, at least part of the way, walked on water (John 6:15–25). The story regarding the manna continues in John 6:26–27:

> Truly, truly, I say to you, you seek me, not because you saw signs, but because you ate the loaves and were filled. Do not work for the food, which perishes, but for the food which endures to eternal life, which the Son shall give to you, for on him the Father, even God, has set his seal.

The people then asked Jesus a question about what they could do to perform the works of God. Jesus answered, "This is the work of God, that you believe in Him Whom He has sent" (v. 29). The people then asked Jesus to show them a sign: "Our fathers ate manna in the wilderness; as it is written, he gave them bread out of heaven to eat" (v. 31). Jesus replied:

> "Truly, truly, I say to you, it is not Moses who has given you the bread out of heaven, but it is my Father who gives you the true bread out of heaven. For the bread of God is that which comes down out of heaven and gives life to the world." When the people heard this they said: "Lord, evermore give us this bread." (vv. 32–33)

Jesus continued: "I am the bread of life; he who comes to me shall not hunger, and he who believes in me shall never thirst" (v. 35). This caused quite a stir among the Jews who heard this, and they began to complain to Jesus because they did not understand. Jesus told them not to grumble among themselves, and he again stated:

> I am the bread of life. Your fathers ate the manna in the wilderness and they died. This is the bread, which comes down out of heaven, so that one may eat of it and not die. I am the living bread that came down out of heaven; if anyone eats of this bread, he shall live forever; and the bread also which I shall give for the life of the world is my flesh. (6:48–51)

Jesus fulfilled this promise at the Last Supper, his last Passover meal, when he told his disciples after giving them the bread, "This is My body which is given for you; do this in remembrance of Me" (Luke 22:19b).

THE CLOUD AND THE ROCK

When the Israelites were in the wilderness, God gave them a pillar of cloud to guide them by day and a pillar of fire to lead them at night (Exodus 13:21). In Paul's first letter to the Corinthian church, he instructed them that the things that happened to the Israelites in the desert were examples for Christian believers.

For I do not want you to be unaware, brethren, that our fathers were all under the cloud, and all passed through the sea; and all were baptized into Moses in the cloud and in the sea; and all ate the same spiritual food; and all drank the same spiritual drink, for they were drinking from a spiritual rock which followed them; and the rock was Christ. Nevertheless, with most of them God was not well-pleased; for they were laid low in the wilderness. Now these things happened as examples for us, that we should not crave evil things, as they also craved. (10:1-6)

Paul added emphasis to this in verses 11-12 of the same chapter:

> Now these things happened to them as an example, and they were written for our instruction, upon whom the ends of the ages have come. Therefore let him who thinks he stands take heed lest he fall.

In other words, the cloud in the wilderness and the rock from which the water came are God-given images that ultimately point to Jesus Christ. It is only in him that we truly "live and move and have our being" (Acts 17:28).

WATER FROM THE ROCK

The people often complained to Moses that they had no water to drink (Exodus 17). Moses cried out to the Lord in despair, and God instructed him to take his staff and strike the rock. Moses did so in the sight of the elders, and water came forth from the rock.

As related in Numbers 20, the Lord instructed Moses to take his rod and speak to the rock so that water would come forth. However, instead of speaking to the rock as God commanded, Moses again struck the rock, this time twice. For this act of disobedience, the Lord told Moses that he would not enter the land of Canaan. In a powerful spiritual sense, the rock represents Christ. Isaiah declares:

> Surely our griefs he himself bore, and our sorrows he carried; yet we ourselves esteemed him stricken, smitten of God, and afflicted. But he was pierced through for our transgressions, he was crushed for our iniquities; the chastening for our well-being fell upon him, and by his scourging we are healed. (53:4–5)

Similarly, Psalm 118:22–23 states, "The stone which the builders rejected has become the chief cornerstone. This is the Lord's doing; It is marvelous in our eyes." Jesus refers to this Psalm in Luke 20:17 when he asks, "What then is this that is written, 'The stone which the builders rejected, this has become the chief cornerstone'?"

In essence, Christ, as the rock in the wilderness and also as the chief cornerstone that the builders rejected, has been stricken once for all time and for all people. Now believers must speak to him, as Moses was instructed to speak to the rock, and call upon his name to experience salvation. There are negative consequences of not surrendering to the Lord. In John 8:24,

Jesus proclaims, "I said therefore to you, that you shall die in your sins; for unless you believe that I am He (the Savior and Messiah of the world), you shall die in your sins."

THE FIERY SERPENTS AND THE BRONZE SERPENT

Having already explained the fact that Christ became our Passover Lamb (1 Corinthians 5:7), there is another story from the book of Numbers that merits attention. Numbers 21 recounts the story of the fiery serpents. The people again complained to God and Moses, saying, "Why have you brought us up out of Egypt to die in this wilderness? For there is no food and no water, and we loathe this miserable food" (speaking of the manna) (v. 5).

In judgment, the Lord sent serpents that bit the people, resulting in many deaths. The people then came to Moses, admitted that they had sinned against God, and asked Moses to intercede for them before the Lord. The Lord instructed Moses to make a bronze serpent and put it on a pole so that those who were bitten by serpents could look upon it and be healed (vv. 6–9).[2]

Figure 3.5 – Staff of Asclepius (courtesy of Sarah Peil Winstead).

This seems to contradict the Second Commandment: "You shall not make for yourself any carved image, or any likeness of anything that is in heaven above, or that is in the earth beneath, or that is in the water under the earth; you shall not bow down to them nor serve them" (Exodus 20:4–5a). God makes an exception to the rule in this case. In the Second Commandment, and in other places in the Old Testament, "second" may represent a picture of Jesus the Messiah as the second person of the Trinity.[3] It is Jesus who explains why God instructed them to look upon a bronze serpent.

Over fourteen centuries later, the meaning becomes clear. In John 3, Nicodemus, a ruler of the Jews, comes to Jesus by night to ask some questions. Jesus first tells him that he must be "born again" to be able to "see the kingdom of God." (John 3:3). Jesus then gives the ultimate answer for the serpent on the pole.

And as Moses lifted up the serpent in the wilderness, even so must the Son of Man be lifted up; that whoever believes may in Him have eternal life. (John 3:14–15)[4]

Bronze represents judgment, and the serpent represents sin. The point is that in Christ, the judgment of God has been met. Christ has taken sin upon himself and suffered the punishment of death so that all who believe in him may be forgiven and have eternal life.

DEUTERONOMY 9:11

> *And it came about at the end of forty days and nights that*
> *the Lord gave me the two tablets of stone, the tablets*
> *of the covenant.*

Deuteronomy literally means "second law." The book consists of three sermons that Moses delivered to the people of Israel while they were camped on the plains of Moab, east of the Jordan River, just before they entered the land of Canaan, the Promised Land. Moses wrote Deuteronomy at Shittim, or Abel-Shittim (Joshua 2:1, 3:1; Numbers 25:1). This is likely to be identified as Tall el-Hammam, a site we helped to excavate.[5]

Figure 3.6 – Tall el-Hammam, the likely site of Shittim (photo by Dr. David E. Graves, ECM).

The Hebrew title is taken from the first words recorded in the book and means "These are the words." This is a more apt title.

The book is not merely a "second law," but a record of Moses's sermons (or explanations) on the law. Also, it reminds the Hebrews of what God did for them in the desert: he delivered them from slavery in Egypt and led them to become a nation, which he founded and kept. In a broad sense, the book renews and reviews the covenant promises that God made with his people at Mount Sinai thirty-nine years prior, around 1446 B.C.

In Deuteronomy 1:6–4:40, Moses reminds the Israelites how the Lord has fought for them and has been with them throughout their wilderness journey. This is the primary point of chapter three. In chapter four, Moses gives several exhortations and reminds the people of the covenant that God made with them at Mt. Sinai. They are cautioned to watch themselves carefully and to not fall into worshipping idols of the nations that they would be conquering. This is addressed in Deuteronomy 4:20–24.

Moses goes on to say that if the people do not obey God, if they act corruptly and do evil in his sight, then God will be provoked to anger, and they will be scattered among the nations. However, God never gives a word of judgment without following it with a word of promise and restoration:

> But from there you will seek the Lord your God, and you will find him, if you search for him with all your heart and all your soul. When you are in distress and all these things come upon you, in the latter days, you will return to the Lord your God and listen to His voice. For the Lord your God is a compassionate God; he will not fail you nor destroy you nor forget the covenant with your fathers, which he swore to them. (4:29–31)

In Deuteronomy 5, Moses begins his second address, and this continues through chapter 26. The Ten Commandments are repeated, and Moses reminds the people that after hearing the voice of God and seeing his fire on the mountain, they asked him to intercede on their behalf so they would not be consumed and die in the presence of God. God tells Moses that the people spoke well: "Oh that they had such a heart in them, that they would fear me, and keep all my commandments always, that it may be well with them and with their sons forever!" (Deuteronomy 5:29)

A review of chapter six brings readers to the heart of Judaism. Verses 4 and 5 represent the Jewish people's statement of faith, their belief in the One True God. This is known as the Shema, which, in Hebrew, means "to hear," or more specifically, "to listen with the intent to obey." "Hear, O Israel: The Lord our God, the Lord *is* one! You shall love the Lord your God with all your heart, with all your soul, and with all your strength."

In Mark 12:29–31, Jesus quotes this verse when he replies to one of the scribes regarding the most important commandment:

> The first of all the commandments *is:* 'Hear, O Israel, the Lord our God, the Lord is one. And you shall love the Lord your God with all your heart, with all your soul, with all your mind, and with all your strength.' This *is* the first commandment. And the second, like *it, is* this: 'You shall love your neighbor as yourself.' There is no other commandment greater than these.[6]

When Jesus was tempted by the devil in the wilderness, he quoted directly from three passages in Deuteronomy:

1. "Man shall not live by bread alone but by everything that proceeds out of the mouth of the Lord" (Matthew 4:4 and Deuteronomy 8:3).
2. "You shall not put the Lord your God to the test" (Matthew 4:7 and Deuteronomy 6:16)."

3. "Worship the Lord your God, and him only shall you serve" (Matthew 4:10b and Deuteronomy 6:13).

There is another important verse in Deuteronomy that is quoted in the New Testament. Deuteronomy 18:15 states, "The Lord your God will raise up for you a prophet like me from among you, from your country-men, you shall listen to him." Stephen quotes this verse in Acts 7:37 in his defense of the Gospel before the Sanhedrin, the Jewish council, before becoming the first Christian martyr.

When Moses speaks of the tablets of the covenant in Deuteronomy 9:11, he is speaking of the Ten Commandments that God gave him on Mt. Sinai. According to Jewish tradition, they were given to Moses fifty days after the Israelites had been freed from slavery in Egypt. This became known as the Feast of Weeks, or the Feast of Pentecost, meaning fifty.

This is the feast of the Lord that the first followers of Christ celebrate when the Holy Spirit is poured out on them in Acts 2. Similar things happened to those believers as what was recorded as happening on Mt. Sinai. After the Holy Spirit descends amid several supernatural phenomena, Peter stands up and gives an explanation, quoting Joel 2:28–32. He then gives a short sermon in which he proclaims that Jesus, through his death, burial, and resurrection, has been made by God to be both Lord and Christ. When the people ask what they are to do, Peter responds:

Repent, and let each of you be baptized in the name of Jesus Christ for the forgiveness of your sins; and you shall receive the gift of the Holy Spirit. For the promise is for you and your children, and for all who are far off, as many as the Lord our God shall call to himself. (Acts 2:38–39)

The tablets of covenant of Deuteronomy 9:11 refer to the law of God written on tablets of stone by the finger of God (Exodus 31:18). As mentioned previously, the prophet Jeremiah spoke of a new covenant that God would make with man:

> "Behold, days are coming," declares the Lord, "when I will make a new covenant with the house of Israel and with the house of Judah, not like the covenant which I made with their fathers in the day I took them by the hand to bring them out of the land of Egypt. My covenant which they broke, although I was a husband to them," declares the Lord. "But this is the covenant which I will make with the house of Israel after those days," declares the Lord. "I will put my law within them, and on their heart I will write it; and I will be their God, and they shall be my people." (Jeremiah 31:31–33)

The prophet Ezekiel put it this way: "Moreover, I will give you a new heart and put a new spirit within you; and I will remove the heart of stone from your flesh and give you a heart of flesh. And I will put My Spirit within you and cause you to walk in my statutes" (Ezekiel 11:19–20a). The apostle Paul clarified this in his second letter to the church at Corinth, writing:

> You are our letter, written in our hearts, known and read by all men; being manifested that you are a letter of Christ, cared for by us, written not with ink, but by the Spirit of the living God, not on tablets of stone but on the tablets of human hearts. (3:2–3)

Deuteronomy 9:11 finds ultimate fulfillment when Jesus, through the Holy Spirit, writes his law on believers' hearts.

AMOS 9:11

> On that day I will raise up the tabernacle of David, which
> has fallen down. And repair its damages; I will raise
> up its ruins, and rebuild it as in the days of old; 12
> that they may possess the remnant of Edom, and all
> the Gentiles who are called by My name,' says the Lord
> who does this thing.

Amos begins by describing himself as a herdsman of Tekoa in
Judah, a small town about twelve miles south of Jerusalem. He
was appointed by God to prophesy against the northern
kingdom, which had become vile and corrupt under King
Jeroboam's rule. He says of himself in 7:14, "I was no prophet,
nor was I the son of a prophet, but I was a herdsman and a
tender of sycamore fruit." Yet God had a strong call on his life,
and he was faithful to that call.

As a whole, the book is broken down into four divisions: eight
prophecies (1:1–2:16), three sermons (3:1–6:14), five visions
(7:1–9:10) and five promises (9:11–15).

This focus verse is extremely important for New Testament
believers because it is referenced and quoted in Acts 15:15–17.
Acts 15 records a debate in the early church over what laws the
early Gentile believers should be required to follow. Certain men
(Jewish men from Judea, a sect of the Pharisees) taught that
unless the Gentile believers were circumcised and followed the
law of Moses, they could not be saved (v. 5). Paul and Barnabas
strongly opposed their position, and a dispute arose among
them over this matter, so a council was called in Jerusalem to
consider this point of argument in the early church. This
became the first recorded church council, and it centered around
the principle presented in Amos 9:11. This meeting took place

in Jerusalem around 49 B.C. and included apostles and elders in the early church.

Acts 15:7 states, "And when there had been much dispute, Peter rose up and said to them, 'Men and brethren, you know that a good while ago God chose among us, that by my mouth the Gentiles should hear the word of the gospel and believe.'" This probably occurred about ten years earlier, around A.D. 39. Verses 8–10 continue, "So God, who knows the heart, acknowledged them by giving them the Holy Spirit just as He did to us, and made no distinction between us and them, purifying their hearts by faith. Now therefore, why do you test God by putting a yoke on the neck of the disciples which neither our fathers nor we were able to bear?" Next, Verse 11 concludes with one of the key verses in the New Testament, stating, " But we believe that through the grace of the Lord Jesus Christ we shall be saved in the same manner as they." This principle is repeated throughout the New Testament and becomes a foundational truth for the Gospel of the Lord Jesus Christ.

Finally, Paul and Barnabas speak up, recounting how many miracles and wonders God worked through them among the Gentiles (v. 12). It is at this point that James, the half brother of Jesus and the recognized leader of the church in Jerusalem, refers to our focus verse, Amos 9:11–12.

The conclusion is then reached that no additional burden or "trouble" should be placed on the Gentiles regarding circumcision or requiring them to keep the law of Moses. The apostle Paul would later write to the church in Corinth in 2 Corinthians 3:2–3, saying, "You are our epistle written in our hearts, known and read by all men; you are manifestly an epistle of Christ, ministered by us, written not with ink but by the Spirit of the living God, not on tablets of stone but on tablets of flesh, that is, of the heart."

The final act of the council was to compose a letter that was to be hand-delivered by Paul, Barnabas, and other leading men of the church to the believers in Antioch and then to all the churches. The message of the letter was given in Acts 15:23–29. The concluding two verses state:

> For it seemed good to the Holy Spirit, and to us to lay upon you no greater burden than these necessary things: that you abstain from things offered to idols, from blood, from things strangled, and from sexual immorality. If you keep yourselves from these, you will do well.

Amos 9:11–12 stands, therefore, as a central verse that unifies the principle of God's covenant with man by making a distinction between the Mosaic Covenant given at Mount Sinai and the New Covenant established in the finished work of Christ and received by faith in His name.

ZECHARIAH 9:11

> *As for you also, because of the blood of your covenant, I*
> *will set your prisoners free from the waterless pit.*

This verse evidently refers back to the blood of the covenant that God established with Abraham as recorded in Genesis 15:9–12. At that time, God promised to give the land of Canaan to Abraham and his descendants. This is an everlasting covenant, and it extends the promise of God to the present day.

The shedding of blood, indicating the seriousness of the covenant bond, is common to all of the biblical covenants. (As Chapter Two of this book points out, the shedding of blood was required in each of the covenants established by God.) The ultimate blood sacrifice, established by Christ in the New Covenant, was fulfilled when Christ died on the cross.

The writer of Hebrews further clarifies this truth in Hebrews 9:12–15:

> Not with the blood of goats and calves, But with His own blood He entered the most Holy Place once for all, For if the blood of bulls and goats and the ashes of a heifer, sprinkling the unclean, sanctifies for the purifying of the flesh, how much more shall the blood of Christ, who through the eternal Spirit offered Himself without spot to God, purge your conscience from dead works to serve the living God. And for this reason He is the mediator of the New Covenant, by means of death, for the redemption of the transgressions under the first covenant that those who are called may receive the promise of the eternal inheritance.

The author of Hebrews then goes on to explain that the Mosaic covenant was also dedicated with blood. Moses ratified the covenant with blood when he sprinkled it on the altar he had built at the base of the mountain. He then read from the book of the covenant (the law which God had given at Mt. Sinai), sprinkled the remaining blood on the people, and said, "Behold, the blood of the covenant which the Lord has made with you according to all these words" (Exodus 24:8)" Hebrews further states in 9:22b that "without the shedding of blood there is no remission," speaking of sin.

The second half of Zechariah 9:11 states that God "will set your prisoners free from the waterless pit." A more literal meaning is that "God will set you free from a cistern that holds no water."

It is interesting to note that there are two important people in the Old Testament who were rescued out of cisterns that held no water. One was Joseph, who was let down into a waterless cistern by his brothers prior to them deciding to sell him to Midianite slave traders, who then took him to Egypt (Genesis 37:28). Jeremiah, the prophet, was the second person left in a waterless cistern. His cistern was actually filled with mud, but he was subsequently rescued as the result of an order given by King Zedekiah (Jeremiah 38:6).

In Jeremiah's first sermon, he declares, "for my people have committed two evils: They have forsaken Me, the fountain of living waters, and hewn themselves cisterns – broken cisterns that can hold no water" (Jeremiah 2:13). In a very real sense, and in a practical application, the pit or cistern that holds no water represents our lives that are born in sin. David says in Psalm 51:5, "Behold, I was brought forth in iniquity, and in sin my mother conceived me." The universal problem for all mankind is that since the fall of Adam and Eve in the garden, we are all born into sin. The enemy of our souls tries to get us to either not admit or to hide from the fact that we are all sinners. The clear solution is to recognize this fact and to call upon the name of the only one who can save us and free us from our helpless state.

Romans 5:8 states, "But God demonstrates His own love toward us, in that while we were yet sinners Christ died for us." The promise given to all in Romans 10:13 claims, "For whoever calls on the name of the Lord shall be saved." Ultimately, there is only one who can deliver us from the pit of sin and despair. His name is Jesus. He is standing by and is quick to hear and deliver the one who, in sincerity and truth, calls on His name.

LINKING OLD AND NEW 9:11 VERSES

When Jesus was teaching His sermon on the Mount, as recorded in Matthew 5–7 and Luke 6:20–26, one of the important things that He pointed out was in Matthew 5:17, where He states, "Do not think that I came to destroy the Law or the Prophets. I did not come to destroy but to fulfill."

He went on to say that everything that was spoken of in the law and the prophets, even to the smallest detail, would ultimately be fulfilled. The first five books of the Bible are known as the Torah and came out of the instructions given to Moses when he received the Law of God on Mt. Sinai. The basic meaning of "Torah" is "instruction." When this concept is kept in focus, one can view the Bible, in a literal sense, as "God's Instruction Manual for Life."

Secondly, the meaning for "Torah" is derived from an archery term that means "to hit the mark" (www. torahresourcesinternational.com). Because of our old, sinful nature, it is virtually impossible for any of us to hit the mark of perfection that the law lays out before us; however, that is where the good news of the gospel comes to our rescue. God sent His Son to be our redeemer, savior, and friend. Because Jesus was born of a virgin, his sinful nature was bypassed by Father God, and he was enabled to live a sinless life and become God's perfect sacrifice for the sins of all mankind. Second Corinthians 5:21 states, "For He made Him who knew no sin to be sin for us, so that we might become the righteousness of God in Him."

A wonderful thing happens when we become followers of Christ. He takes our sin upon himself and imputes to us his righteousness. Through the power of the Holy Spirit, we become partakers of his divine nature. That is not to say that as followers of Christ, we do not sin, because we still do, but when we confess our sins to God, he continues to forgive us and to cleanse us of all unrighteousness (1 John 1:9).

Ephesians 2:8–10 speaks of the wonderful and unmerited favor of God that is extended to us through his Son: "For by grace you have been saved through faith, and that not of yourselves; it is the gift of God, not of works, lest anyone should boast. For we are His workmanship created in Christ Jesus for good works, which God prepared beforehand that we should walk in them."

The Old Testament passages that require sacrifices for forgiveness of sins were all fulfilled in and through the final atoning work of Christ on the cross. He is the Lamb of God, who takes away the sins of the world (John 1:29). When He appears again, he will come as the lion of the tribe of Judah, the root of David. The remainder of the unfilled prophecies in the Bible will find their consummation in Him, and He will forever reign as King of Kings and Lord of Lords (Revelation 5:5).

In his letter to the church in Rome, Paul wrote about this covenant theme running through the entirety of Scripture:

For I do not desire, brethren, that you should be ignorant of this mystery, lest you should be wise in your own opinion, that hardening in part has happened to Israel until the fullness of the Gentiles has come in. And so all Israel will be saved, as it is written: "And He will turn away ungodliness from Jacob; for this is My covenant with them, when I take away their sins." (Romans 11:25–27)

Jesus fulfilled all of the covenant promises made to Israel and to mankind.

4

SOMEONE CALL 9:11 - PART TWO: THE NEW TESTAMENT

OUR ATTENTION NOW TURNS TO THE NEW TESTAMENT 9:11 Scriptures, focusing on the verses and the chapters in which they are found to ensure appropriate context. This is important when studying Scripture so that focus is not only on the "then and there," what was spoken to that particular group of people then, but also on the "here and now;" the practical application to life today.

MATTHEW 9:11

> *And when the Pharisees saw this, they said to His*
> *disciples, "Why does your teacher eat with tax*
> *gatherers and sinners?"*

Matthew 9 begins with a story of Jesus healing a man brought to him by his friends. The parallel accounts, Mark 2:1–12 and Luke 5:17–26, indicate that it was so crowded where Jesus was teaching that the friends lowered the paralyzed man down through the roof. In Luke 5:19, the Greek word used for tiles is "keramos," meaning "ceramic." This was an expensive roof that was destroyed to get this lame man to Jesus.

Archaeological finds suggest that the use of tiles for private houses in the first century was quite rare. Ongoing excavations at contemporary sites such as Khirbet el-Maqatir, Khirbet Cana, Magdala, Modiin, and Bethsaida may provide insight on how widespread ceramic roofs were in the first century.

Figure 4.1 – Roofing Tile from Khirbet el-Maqatir (photo by Michael Luddeni).

Matthew provides us with an account of this story:

> When Jesus saw their faith, he said, "Take courage my son, your sins are forgiven." Scribes, Pharisees, and teachers of the law were present and reasoned among themselves, "This fellow blasphemes." Jesus, however, knew their thoughts and said, "Why are you thinking evil in your hearts? For which is easier, to say, 'Your sins are forgiven,' or to say, 'Rise, and walk'." "But in order that you may know that the Son of Man has authority

on earth to forgive sins." Then he said to the paralytic, "Rise, take up your bed and go home." When those in attendance saw this, "they were filled with awe, and glorified God" (Matthew 9:2–8).

Immediately following this (9:9), Jesus passed by and, upon seeing Matthew (called Levi in the books of Mark and Luke), simply said to him, "Follow me." He then had dinner in Matthew's home, inviting a number of his friends, including tax collectors and sinners.

Matthew 9:11 demonstrates Jesus's offer of redemption and forgiveness to sinners and his willingness to enter their homes and lives. When the Pharisees saw this, they asked his disciples, "Why does your Teacher eat with the tax-gatherers and sinners?" Jesus responded:

> It is not those who are healthy who need a physician, but those who are ill, but go and learn what this means, "I desire compassion, and not sacrifice, for I did not come to call the righteous, but sinners." (9:12–13)

Jesus was alluding to Hosea 6:6 when he added, "For I desire mercy, not sacrifice, and the knowledge of God more that burnt offerings."[1]

MARK 9:11

> *And they began questioning Him saying, "Why is it that the scribes say that first Elijah must come?"*

This verse must be understood in the context of verses 1–13, which speak of the transfiguration of Christ. Jesus's transfiguration is also recorded in Matthew 16:28–17:3 and in Luke 9:27–36. Peter also wrote about it in 2 Peter 1:17–18.

Preceding this event, each of the Gospel authors tells of Peter's confession of faith, Jesus's teaching on the costs of discipleship, and finally, Jesus speaking about his return (Greek – "parousia").

For what does it profit a man to gain the whole world, and forfeit his soul? For what shall a man give in exchange for his soul? For whoever is ashamed of me and my words in this adulterous and sinful generation, the Son of Man will also be ashamed of him when he comes in the glory of his Father with the holy angels. (Mark 8:36–38)

Mark 9 begins with Jesus saying, "Truly I say to you, there are some of those who are standing here who shall not taste of death until they see the kingdom of God after it has come with power." Then, after six days passed, Jesus took Peter, James, and John with him up to a high mountain and was transfigured before them.

Luke explains that this happened while Jesus prayed and that his face was altered. Matthew states, "His face shone like the sun, and his garments became as white as the light" (Matthew 17:2). Mark adds that Elijah appeared with Moses and they were both talking to Jesus. Luke reports that they were talking to Jesus about his imminent death in Jerusalem. Peter spoke up and said that they should make three booths, or tabernacles – one for Jesus, one for Elijah, and one for Moses. A cloud encompassed them, and from out of the cloud, they heard a voice saying, "This is my beloved Son, listen to Him!" (Mark 9:7)

Suddenly, they found themselves alone, and only Jesus was standing with them. As they came down from the mountain,

Jesus commanded them to tell no one what had happened or what they had seen until after the Son of Man (Daniel 7:13–14) had risen from the dead. They obeyed his word but questioned what he meant when he said he would "rise from the dead."

In Mark 9:11, the disciples ask him, "Why is it that the scribes say that first Elijah must come?" (referencing Malachi 4:5, which says, "Behold, I am going to send you Elijah the prophet before the coming of the great and terrible day of the Lord"). Jesus answers them in Mark 9:12–13:

> Elijah does first come and restore everything. And yet how is it written of the Son of Man that He should suffer many things and be treated with contempt? But I say to you that Elijah has indeed come, and they did to him whatever they wished, just as it is written of him.

Jesus is clearly referring to John the Baptist (Matthew 11:14). Many such prophecies find fulfillment in the New Testament. Dozens of Old Testament prophecies were fulfilled in Jesus Christ, some of which can be found in Psalm 22 and Isaiah 7, 9, 50, and 53.

LUKE 9:11

> *But the multitudes were aware of this and followed him;*
> *and welcoming them, he began speaking to them about*
> *the kingdom of God and curing those who had need of*
> *healing.*

Luke 9 begins with Jesus giving his disciples the authority to cast out demons and heal diseases. He then sends them out to proclaim the Kingdom of God (Luke 9:1–2). He also instructs them:

> Take nothing for your journey, neither a staff, nor a bag, nor bread, nor money; and do not even have two tunics apiece. And whatever house you enter, stay there, and take your leave from there. And as for those who do not receive you, when you depart from that city, shake off the dust from your feet as a testimony against them. (9:3–5)

The disciples did as Jesus told them. When Herod the tetrarch heard what was happening, he was greatly perplexed because some were saying that John the Baptist had risen from the dead (Herod had had John the Baptist beheaded sometime before this), that Elijah had appeared, or that one of the prophets of old had returned. Herod said, "I myself had John beheaded; but who is this man about whom I hear such things?" (Luke 9:9) and he continued trying to see Jesus.

Figure 4.2 – Machaerus, where John the Baptist was beheaded (photo by Dr. David E. Graves, ECM).

The disciples returned to Jesus, and they told him what had occurred. Jesus then took them to a deserted place near the city of Bethsaida. Multitudes also followed him (v. 11).

Luke 9:11 speaks of the power that Christ holds over sickness and demons and of the power that he gives to those who follow him: "But the multitudes were aware of this and followed him; and welcoming them, he began speaking to them about the kingdom of God and curing those who had need of healing." Parallel accounts are found in the other synoptic Gospels: Matthew 10:1–14; 14:1–14; Mark 6:7–16; 30–34.

JOHN 9:11

> *He answered, "The man who is called Jesus made clay, and*
> *anointed my eyes, and said to me, 'Go to Siloam, and*
> *wash;' so I went away and washed, and I received*
> *sight."*

John 9 tells the story of a blind man's healing. When the disciples saw this man who had been born blind, they asked Jesus, "Rabbi, who sinned, this man or his parents, that he should be born blind?" Jesus replied:

> It was neither that this man sinned, nor his parents; but it was
> in order that the works of God might be displayed in him. We
> must work the works of him who sent me, as long as it is day;
> night is coming, when no man can work. While I am in the
> world, I am the light of the world. (John 9:3–5)

John's Gospel is different from the synoptic Gospels in that it focuses more on the deity of Christ. As the unique, only begotten Son of the Father, he was fully man and fully God. The deity of Christ is spoken of in John 1:1–5:

> In the beginning was the Word, and the Word was with God, and the Word was God [Word = Greek Logos = Jesus Christ]. He was in the beginning with God. All things came into being by him; and apart from him; nothing came into being that has come into being. In him was life; and the life was the light of men. And the light shines in the darkness; and the darkness did not comprehend it.

John's Gospel presents seven miracles and seven "I Am" statements by Christ.

The seven miracles recorded in John are as follows

1. Turning water into wine – John 2:1–12
2. Healing the nobleman's son – John 4:46–54
3. Healing a lame man at the Pool of Bethesda – John 5:1–17
4. The feeding of the five thousand – John 6:1–14
5. Walking on water – John 6:16–21
6. Healing the man born blind – John 9:1–12
7. The raising of Lazarus from the dead – John 11:1–46

Note: Some would also include the post-resurrection miracle of the draught of fish.

When Jesus spoke of himself as the "I Am," he was saying that he is one with the Father (i.e., the same one who spoke to Moses out of the burning bush and called himself "I Am," as told in Exodus 3:14). Jesus said, "I and the Father are one" (John 10:30). When the disciple Philip asked Jesus to reveal the Father, Jesus replied, "He who has seen Me has seen the Father" (John 14:8–9).

The seven primary "I Am" statements of John are:

1. I am the bread of life – John 6:35
2. I am the light of the world – John 8:12 and 9:5
3. I am the door of the sheep – John 10:7, 9
4. I am the good shepherd – John 10:11,14
5. I am the resurrection and the life – John 11:25
6. I am the way, the truth, and the life – John 14:6
7. I am the true vine – John 15:1, 5

Jesus proclaimed, "Truly, truly, I say to you, the Son can do nothing of himself, unless it is something he sees the Father doing; for whatever the Father does, these things the Son does in like manner" (John 5:19).

He also confirmed his deity to a man he healed of blindness:

"Do you believe in the Son of Man?" The man answered and said, "And who is he Lord, that I may believe in him?" Jesus said to him, "You have both seen him and he is the one who is talking with you." And he said, "Lord I believe." And he worshipped him. (John 9:35–38)

Figure 4.3 – Pool of Siloam: Here Jesus healed a man's blindness (photo by Steven Rudd).

The 9:11 verses within the four Gospel accounts portray Jesus as a friend of sinners, one whose coming was preceded by a herald, John the Baptist, one who was transfigured in the presence of several of his select disciples, and one who healed and delivered many, even a person born blind. Jesus sent forth his disciples to proclaim God's covenant of mercy to all who call on the name of Christ.

ACTS 9:11–12

> And the Lord said to him, "Arise and go to the street called
> Straight, and inquire at the house of Judas for a man
> from Tarsus named Saul, for behold, he is praying, and
> he has seen in a vision a man named Ananias come in

and lay his hands on him, so that he might regain his sight."

Acts 9 is one of the best-known passages in the New Testament. It is the account of a Pharisee, Saul of Tarsus, and his powerful conversion on the way to Damascus. Acts 22:4–11 and Acts 26:13–18 also give testimonial accounts regarding Saul's "powerful encounter" with the living Christ. After Saul's conversion experience, his name was changed to Paul, a name that would expedite his missionary travels around the Mediterranean.

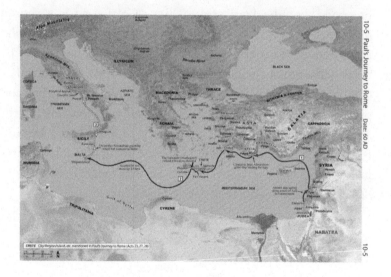

Figure 4.4 – Map of the Mediterranean world (photo by Todd Bolen/Bibleplaces.com).

Before his encounter with Christ, Saul was one of the persecutors of the early Christian Church. He even supervised Stephen's stoning (Acts 7:58). He received letters from the high priest authorizing him to go to the synagogues in Damascus. He arrested any followers of The Way (as the early believers were known) and brought them back to Jerusalem for trial and punishment.

On his way to Damascus, he had an encounter with Jesus that forever changed his life. A bright light knocked him to the ground, rendering him blind. The risen Jesus confronted him over his attacks on the early believers. For the next three days, Saul sought God and fasted.

During this time, the Lord appeared in a vision to Ananias, a disciple. Ananias was instructed to go to Saul, lay hands on him, and pray for him to receive his sight. Initially, Ananias protested, but the Lord said to him, "Go, for he is a chosen instrument of mine, to bear my name before the Gentiles and kings and the sons of Israel; for I will show him how much he must suffer for My name's sake" (Acts 9:15–16). Ananias did as the Lord requested. He went to Saul, laid hands on him, and prayed. Saul regained his sight, was filled with the Holy Spirit, and was baptized in water. Beginning in the second century B.C., devout Jewish believers practiced daily immersion in water in a mikveh, so the house where he was lodging on Straight Street likely had its own mikveh (ritual bath).

Figure 4.5 – Mikveh excavated at Khirbet el-Maqatir by Scott Stripling (photo by Michael Luddeni).

Paul became a great apostle to the nations. He went on three missionary journeys, established many churches, and wrote at least thirteen letters in the New Testament. These are known as the Pauline epistles.

In Paul's testimony, as recorded in Acts 26:17–18, when the Lord appears to him on the Damascus road, he proclaims:

I will deliver you from the Jewish people, as well as from the Gentiles, to whom I now send you, to open their eyes and to turn them from darkness to light, and from the power of Satan to God, that they may receive forgiveness of sins and an inheritance among those who are sanctified by faith in me.

In summary, Acts 9 tells the story of the powerful conversion experience of Saul of Tarsus, who became Paul, the great apostle to the Gentiles. It also speaks of the role of Christ's humble servant Ananias, who was obedient to the purpose for which God called him.

HEBREWS 9:11–12

But when Christ appeared as a high priest of the good things to come, he entered through the greater and more perfect tabernacle, one not made with hands – that is to say, not of this creation – and not through the blood of goats and calves, but through his own blood did he enter the holy place once and for all, having obtained eternal redemption.

In the Old Testament, the blood of the innocent sacrifices that were offered for the cleansing of sins provided only a temporary solution. Sins were covered, not forgiven. But Christ, through his shed blood, now offers a once-and-for-all atonement for the sins of all mankind. This atonement is available for all who will call upon his name.

Hebrews 9:14 states, "How much more will the blood of Christ, who through the eternal Spirit offered Himself without blemish to God, cleanse your conscience from dead works to serve the living God?" Verse 15 continues: "And for this reason He is the mediator of a new covenant." Hebrews 1:1–3 declares:

> God, after He spoke long ago to the fathers in the prophets, in many portions and in many ways, in these last days has spoken to us in his Son, whom he appointed heir of all things, through whom also he made the world. And he is the radiance of his glory and the exact representation of his nature and upholds all things by the word of His power. When he had made purification of sins, he sat down at the right hand of the Majesty on high.

Hebrews presents Christ as the one who has become "the Apostle and High Priest of our confession" (3:1). He has been counted worthy of more glory than Moses. Moses was faithful in his house as a servant, but Christ is faithful as a Son over his house, or us (Hebrews 3:3–6). The writer of Hebrews also cautions believers to not fall away from the faith:

> Take care, brethren, lest there should be in any one of you an evil, unbelieving heart, in falling away from the living God. But encourage one another day after day, as long as it is still called today, lest any one of you be hardened by the deceitfulness of sin. (3:12–13)

In Hebrews 9:11, Jesus is referred to as "a high priest of the good things to come," becoming the perfect sacrifice and bringing hope to those who seek him. Hebrews 9:28 concludes by stating, "So Christ also, having been offered once to bear the sins of many, shall appear a second time for salvation without reference to sin, to those who eagerly await Him."

REVELATION 9:11

> *They have as king over them, the angel of the abyss; his*
> *name in Hebrew is Abaddon (destruction), and in the*
> *Greek he has the name Apollyon (destroyer).*

The book of Revelation, or the Apocalypse (which means the unveiling), describes four visions given to John when he was in prison on the island of Patmos (Revelation 1:9). Revelation 1:1 makes clear that this is the "Revelation of Jesus Christ, which God gave him to show to His bond-servants, the things which must shortly take place; and he sent and communicated it by his angel to his bond-servant John." The book of Revelation also promises a blessing to those who read and heed it: "Blessed is he who reads and those who hear the words of the prophecy, and heed the things which are written in it, for the time is near" (1:3).

One of the most obvious symbolic features in Revelation is its reiterated series of sevens. There are letters to seven churches, seven seals of judgment, seven trumpets of judgment, and seven bowls of judgment. The verse of focus occurs with the blowing of the fifth trumpet. In chapter 9, John begins by stating that a fifth angel sounds and that he sees a star, probably representing a fallen angel or possibly even Satan himself, falling from heaven. Luke 10:17–20 is a related passage:

> And the seventy returned with joy, saying, "Lord, even the demons are subject to us in your name." And He said to them, "I was watching Satan fall from heaven like lightning. Behold, I have given you authority to tread upon serpents and scorpions, and over all the power of the enemy, and nothing shall injure you. Nevertheless, do not rejoice in this, that the spirits are

subject to you, but rejoice that your names are recorded in heaven."

In Revelation 9, the bottomless pit is opened:

Smoke went up out of the pit, like the smoke of a great furnace; and the sun and the air were darkened by the smoke of the pit. Then out of the smoke came forth locusts upon the earth; and power was given them, as the scorpions of the earth have power. And they were told that they should not hurt the grass of the earth, nor any green thing, nor any tree, but only the men who do not have the seal of God on their foreheads. (9:2–4)

The only ones protected from the suffering and torment that the locusts bring are the ones who have the seal of God on their foreheads. The suffering resulting from the scorpions is limited to a period of five months. Concerning the seal, Paul explained:

In Him, you also, after listening to the message of truth, the Gospel of your salvation – having also believed, you were sealed in him with the Holy Spirit of promise, who is given as a pledge of our inheritance, with a view to the redemption of God's own possession, to the praise of his glory. (Ephesians 1:13–14)

To understand the plague of locusts, one must look back to Exodus and the plagues that God brought against Pharaoh and the gods of the Egyptians (See Figure 3.1.). The eighth plague is a plague of locusts. On that occasion, the locusts covered the surface of the whole land so that it was darkened, and they ate every green thing and all the fruit that was left on the trees after the hail. Pharaoh called Moses and Aaron and said, "I have sinned against the Lord your God and against you. Now therefore, please forgive my sin only this once, and make supplication to the Lord your God, that he would only remove this death from me" (Exodus 10:15–20). Moses did as Pharaoh requested, and the Lord brought forth a strong west wind that drove the locusts into the Red Sea, but then the Lord hardened Pharaoh's heart so that he did not let the people of Israel go.

There would only be one more plague, three days of total darkness, before the final plague, the death of the firstborn. The angel of death, sent forth by God, is referred to as the destroyer. Exodus 12:23 reads:

> For the Lord will pass through to smite the Egyptians; and when he sees the blood on the lintel and on the two doorposts, the Lord will pass over the door and will not allow the destroyer to come into your houses to smite you.

The only ones protected from the destroyer in Revelation 9:11 are those with the seal of God on their foreheads. They are the ones who have put their faith and trust in the finished work of Christ on the cross. In Galatians 3:13, Paul wrote: "Christ redeemed us from the curse of the Law, having become a curse for us for it is written, 'Cursed is everyone who hangs on a tree'" (see Deuteronomy 21:23).

Similarly, Paul wrote in Romans 5:8–9:

> But God demonstrates His own love toward us, in that while we were yet sinners, Christ died for us. Much more then, having now been justified by his blood, we shall be saved from the wrath of God through Him.

Revelation 9:11 stands as a warning and a loving invitation to receive the free gift of an eternal relationship with the One True Creator through Jesus Christ. The covenant promises throughout the Bible have been completely fulfilled through

Jesus. He is the mediator of a new and better covenant (Hebrews 12:24).

Revelation concludes in 22:12–17:

> "Behold, I am coming quickly, and my reward is with me, to render to every man according to what he has done. I am the Alpha and the Omega, the first and the last, the beginning and the end." Blessed are those who wash their robes, that they may have the right to the tree of life, and may enter by the gates into the city. Outside are the dogs and the sorcerers and the immoral persons and the murderers and the idolaters, and everyone who loves and practices lying. "I, Jesus, have sent my angel to testify to you these things for the churches. I am the root and the offspring of David, the bright morning star." And the Spirit and the bride say, "Come." And let the one who hears say, "Come." And let the one who is thirsty come; let the one who wishes take the water of life without cost.

CONCLUSION OF THE BIBLICAL 9:11 PASSAGES

What an incredible summary in the preceding passages, of the relationship God aims for us to all achieve with him. Not only do we see that God has always used covenants to lovingly woo his people into close relationship with him, for their eternal benefit, we also see that thanks to Jesus, the privilege of establishing a personal covenant relationship with the very Creator God is now freely available to everyone.

Initiating that covenant relationship is the moment we activate God's personal protection, provision and blessing. Needless to say, there is never a bad time to do that, but doing so early in our lives, or as early as possible, means locking in God's presence before "trials and tribulations" make impact. We always end up asking ourselves when the storms of life hit us, how strong are the foundations of my shelter? If we are in a living covenant with God, we can be sure that our foundations are strong enough to withstand every storm that might come our way. That is his promise. In the following chapters we want to share, by way of encouragement and inspiration, how that has played out for each of us.

5

GOD IS IN CONTROL – RALPH'S TESTIMONY

AT A HOME BIBLE STUDY RECENTLY, SOMEONE ASKED the question, "What is your natural age versus your spiritual age?" One man spoke up and said he was thirty-four but, as a practicing Christian, he was only about three. He and his wife began attending church just three years ago. Every Sunday, he felt as though the pastor were speaking directly to him. Ironically, the messages addressed issues he was facing at the time: his spiritual life, marriage, parenting, and work. While he had called himself a Christian for many years, he had only become serious about his faith during the last three years.

This Bible study revolved around the book called *Emotionally Healthy Spirituality* by Pastor Peter Scazzero of New Life Fellowship Church in Queens, New York City. Our pastor had been preaching a sermon series based on this book. A picture of a mostly submerged iceberg graces the book's cover. Similarly, our lives often expose only those areas we choose to reveal, while the submerged parts remain hidden beneath the surface. Thankfully, God, who sees all our hidden parts, is merciful.

Writing this chapter became a spiritual exercise for me as I reflected on my experience of living thirty-one years with limited spiritual growth. Additionally, I knew I risked exposing the hidden messiness of my own personal spiritual journey.

I was in the second grade when my family moved to a country farm located halfway between the small towns of Hockley and Waller, northwest of Houston. Both of my parents grew up in this area and wanted to return there to raise their two sons. My mom was born in a small house just down the road from where we lived. My dad worked as a welder in Houston and commuted forty miles each way, leaving at 4:30 every morning. He loved living in the country and did not mind the long daily drive. Dad also enjoyed farming. We grew corn, which we sold to local dairies. There was always plenty of work to do. Shortly after we moved to the country, my mom returned to college to obtain a teaching certificate. She taught elementary school as well as high school math. My parents were hard workers.

One of my dad's hobbies was calf roping. We always owned a good roping horse, along with plenty of calves, and Dad built a roping pen behind our house. My brother and I enjoyed roping and had fun trying to ride the small calves when we were not roping them. One afternoon after school, we were riding calves as we had done countless times before. Being older, I would hold the calf as my smaller brother stealthily mounted its back. This time, I grabbed a calf with small horns. Larry quickly scurried onto its back, held tight, and in the blink of an eye, flew over the front of it, piercing his right eye on the nub of the calf's horn. Blood flowed from his eye when he stood. Luckily, he had hit the globe portion of his eye and did not lose his sight. We were so frightened that we never rode calves again, and any aspirations we ever had of becoming professional bull riders ended that day. After that, roping dominated our afternoons and weekends. In high school, football, basketball, track, and tennis replaced roping and consumed our time.

My wife, Charlotte, and I grew up attending the same church. Charlotte's parents lived across the street from the church, and she was there whenever the doors opened. My family and I lived further out in the country. I was limited to only attending with my parents on Sunday mornings until I got my driver's license. One of my fondest childhood memories is of standing between my parents on Sunday mornings, hearing my father's baritone voice on one side and my mother's comforting voice on the other as they sang great hymns of faith. It was in that small Baptist church, at the age of nine or ten, that I made a profession of faith and was baptized. I was sincere in my faith walk and enjoyed attending church and Sunday school.

Charlotte and I both grew up in stable, Christian homes. Neither of our parents fought, at least as far as we knew. I do not remember my parents ever saying an unkind word to each other. However, my dad had a serious weakness in his life: a fondness for whiskey. While it was not problematic during my childhood, it eventually surfaced.

Once I got my driver's license, knowing Charlotte would be there, I began attending church on Sunday night. As a teenager, I rededicated my life to the Lord. I did my best to live as a good person, and I absolutely considered myself a Christian. I even sang a solo in a revival service. However, I got so nervous that I decided the choir was a better place for me. I also read my Bible regularly. One verse, in particular, disturbed me: "Therefore, if anyone is in Christ, he is a new creation, old things have passed away; behold all things have become new" (2 Corinthians 5:17).

While other people shared their testimonies, especially missionaries or evangelists who spoke in church, about how the Lord had radically changed their lives when they had become followers of Christ, I could not say that. I struggled with what the Bible had to say about being a new creation in Christ. I finally decided to just accept 2 Corinthians 5:17 by faith and tried not to be overly concerned about it.

Sometimes kids know at an early age what they want to do in life, but I really had no clue. I was a good student and always tried to make A's. My mom wanted me to be an attorney. We had an uncle who was a bankruptcy judge in Houston, and she hoped I might follow in his footsteps; however, I always liked biology and science better. I remained undecided until my senior year of high school, when a dramatic, life-changing event occurred, setting the course for the profession I would ultimately pursue.

Charlotte and I began dating during the summer between our junior and senior years of high school. We had been dating for about six months when her parents called to say that she had been rushed to the local hospital for emergency surgery. She had to have an emergency appendectomy under spinal anesthesia. Our local general physician performed the procedure. Unfortunately, he did not realize that Charlotte's appendix had ruptured before being removed. After about a week of apparent recovery, the pain returned with great intensity.

Suddenly, Charlotte had to be rushed to St. Luke's hospital in Houston's Medical Center, where she again underwent emergency surgery. When I went to visit her in the hospital, she was still in tremendous pain and had tubes running everywhere, with surgical drains coming from her abdomen. As I stood helplessly by her bedside that day, all I wanted to do was help ease her pain and suffering. It was then that I purposed I would never again be helpless regarding her medical care. I decided to become a medical doctor.

When she finally came home, Charlotte looked like she had just been released from a prisoner of war camp, not a hospital. She had gone into the hospital weighing 116 pounds and come out weighing only seventy-nine. At least she was still alive and would recover.

Together we attended Sam Houston State University in Huntsville, Texas. Charlotte majored in elementary education, and I played football and pursued pre-med studies. One of my roommates for two years was Eliseo Villarreal, whom we called Chayo. A two-sport All-American in baseball and football, he also quietly and faithfully demonstrated his devotion to God day in and day out. At that point in my life, I was not reading the Bible daily; however, I clearly remember Chayo continually reading a small copy of the New Testament that he carried in his back pocket. Little did I know that decades later, Chayo would disciple one of his high school athletes named Scott Stripling. Scott would later become a close friend and is the co-author of this book.

Charlotte and I married before our last semester in college. In 1962, on a Sunday afternoon, December 23, we had a Christmas wedding in our hometown church. Charlotte and I moved to Galveston in 1963 after my acceptance into the University of Texas Medical School – Galveston branch. Charlotte taught elementary school in nearby La Marque.

Medical school proved to be the greatest academic challenge I had encountered. I studied until two or three each morning just to keep up with the material the professors covered. The cycle of repeating that schedule day in and day out became exhausting. Before this, A's had come easily in school, but now I had to work diligently to earn every grade. Nevertheless, we enjoyed our four-year stay in Galveston and still possess very fond memories of the friendships created and experiences shared.

I will always remember one afternoon during this grueling time. On Friday, November 22, 1963, I was in gross anatomy lab when someone told us that the president's motorcade had been fired upon in Dallas. We walked across the street to the Old Red bookstore, where we watched the news unfold on television. Walter Cronkite's announcement that President Kennedy had died shocked and numbed us. It was a watershed moment that changed the course of history for the United States and for the world.

The birth of our son, Gary, in 1966, dramatically impacted us in a positive way. Because of Charlotte's previous illness and multiple surgeries, she had a difficult time conceiving a child. In the summer of 1967, during the Vietnam conflict, I interned at the Memorial Hospital System in Houston. In late 1967, it became apparent that to fulfill my military obligation, my only two options were to volunteer or be drafted. After calling my local Navy recruiter, I learned that I would be stationed in Southeast Asia with the Marines for at least a year if I volunteered, so I decided to pursue other options. Fortunately, several of us learned of openings in the U.S. Public Health Service. I was accepted and subsequently stationed at a hospital in Norfolk, Virginia. Our beautiful daughter Cheryl was born just before we moved in June of 1968.

We remained stationed in Norfolk, Virginia, for two years. As soon as we moved and were settled, we began looking for a new church home. Our first Sunday in Norfolk, we visited a Baptist church near our home. They served good coffee and doughnuts before the service; however, the preaching was very different from our previous home church. We expected to hear the same Gospel message we'd grown up hearing, but unfortunately, we learned there are many different approaches to ministry. When the pastor, apparently going through a faith crisis, delivered his sermon, he questioned whether he believed that the Bible was even true. Charlotte and I both agreed that we did not want to attend a church where the pastor would confess publically that he was not even sure if he was a believer. We soon found a church that preached the Gospel as we were accustomed.

My experience in the hospital was like doing a two-year residency in general medicine. We rotated through internal medicine, surgery, orthopedics, and urology. We covered everything except obstetrics. We had excellent staff doctors in every specialty area and learned and grew under their teaching.

Several doctors on staff were committed Christians. I not only learned from their medical practices, but I learned from their spiritual lives as well. They impacted others with their faith, and through them, I saw what good doctors practicing their faith looked like. One day, while I was working with a Jewish doctor, out of the blue, he stated, "You know, Ralph, the chief of internal medicine is such a fine person that he must be a saint." What a statement, and what an example. His life was his witness, as it should be for all who call themselves followers of Christ.

After two years under the direction of these doctors, Charlotte and I returned to Houston, where I began pursuing a career in radiology, which I believed would allow me to pursue my career without compromising precious family time. Diagnostic radiology uses various imaging procedures such as X-rays, CAT scans, nuclear medicine, ultrasound, and MRIs to yield a diagnosis for the patient and referring physician. It remains primarily a hospital-based specialty with fairly regular work hours. This honored a promise I had made to my mom to not let medicine take away from family time.

Upon arriving in Houston, we immediately began seeking another church home. Our close friends, Janis and Dennis Jensen, attended a small Baptist church in the Bellaire area, which is where we also settled. Although we attended church regularly, my spiritual walk and personal relationship with God was lacking. At our new church, I realized quickly that if I did not volunteer to serve in some capacity, someone would surely ask me to serve in another, so I volunteered to help Charlotte teach a fifth-grade Sunday School class. As it turned out, it was the best place for me to be spiritually. Today, Charlotte and I enjoy watching the show *Are You Smarter Than a Fifth Grader?* When I watch the show, I am reminded of that fifth-grade Sunday school class because it was then that God showed me areas in my life that remained spiritually void.

God met me right where I was and connected with me through the teacher of that class. Charlotte had invited a lady, Evelyn, to help teach it. She taught the Bible lesson and loved using scriptural songs, which stuck in my heart. For the next two years, Charlotte and I had the privilege of experiencing Evelyn's teaching. We witnessed her love for the Lord, for the Word of God, and for those fifth-graders. It was a love far deeper than anything I had ever known in my own walk with God.

During this time, our church received a new pastor. Charlotte and I became close, lifelong friends with Jeff and Ruthie Campbell, who greatly influenced our spiritual journey. Charlotte and I had heard hundreds of sermons on how to receive salvation by believing in Christ; however, we had never heard messages on making Christ Lord over our entire lives. As I sat and listened to Jeff's sermons, it was as if the Holy Spirit began a new work in my life. While I looked okay on the outside, I was a mess on the inside. At church, I would often put on my happy face. I would then walk out the door and become angry with my wife and children for no apparent reason. I became sick and tired of being sick and tired.

One day, in desperation, during the invitational time at church, I bowed my head. From the depths of my heart, I prayed this simple prayer: "Lord, I don't know what's wrong with me, but I want to start over with you, and I want to be a New Testament Christian, whatever that means." At that moment, it was as though a light bulb came on in my spirit. Later, I read in Proverbs 20:27: "The Spirit of man is the lamp of the Lord searching all the innermost parts of his being." This is exactly what happened within my own heart and soul that day. God's Holy Spirit came alive within me, and I became a new creation in Christ. This began a process of change in my life. I was no longer haunted by 2 Corinthians 5:17. I began to understand what that verse means by being a new creation.

I became more interested in my personal Bible study. Knowing my previous walk with the Lord was devoid of something, I suddenly had a new excitement whereby Jesus became real in my heart and in my life. As Paul describes in Ephesians 2 and in Colossians 3, I began to "put off the old man and put on the new." This change began in December 1972, just after the birth of our third child, Melissa Kay. Charlotte and the kids began to notice changes where it counted the most, at home. Church members also noticed a change and asked me to become a deacon near the end of 1973. The guy previously hiding out in the fifth-grade Sunday school class had become someone excited about the Lord and his work in my life. I wanted to reread the New Testament and focus on the red letters, the words spoken by Christ. I knew that I would not comprehend or understand all that he had said, but I wanted to grow in my knowledge of him and his words. I began every Bible study session with this prayer: "Lord, open my heart to understand your Word."

Two men from our church's deacon board interviewed me for the deacon position. I considered these men the godliest on the board. I had already made it through the book of Acts, reading that the leaders in the early church had been men filled with the Holy Spirit. That night, I asked these two men, "How do I know if I am filled with the Holy Spirit?" They told me that everyone who believes in Christ and is born again has the Holy Spirit within them. At first, their answer satisfied me; however, the book of Acts makes a clear distinction between those believers filled with the Spirit and those who are not. I reasoned that if all believers were Spirit-filled Christians, they would not be satisfied just sitting in the pew every Sunday as I had been doing for so long. If filled with the Spirit, they would be on fire for God, and that fire would be evident in their lives.

I reread John 14. Jesus tells his disciples not to be troubled: "You believe in God, believe also in me." He then states that he is going away to prepare a place for them and that if he goes away, then he will come back and "receive them unto Himself." In verse 4, Jesus says, "And where I go you know, and the way you know." The disciples had a hard time understanding what Jesus was saying to them. Thomas says, "Lord, we do not know where you are going, so how can we know the way?" Then, in verses 6–7, Jesus replies, "I am the way and the truth and the life. No one comes to the Father but through me. If you had known me, you would have known my Father also; and from now on you know him and have seen him."

Still confused, Philip asks, "Lord, show us the Father, and it is enough for us." I thought to myself as I read verse 5, "Wow, the disciples had been with the Lord for three or so years. They had seen all the miracles. They had heard the incredible teaching. They had seen the blind regain their sight, the deaf regain their hearing, and the dead brought back to life." Even so, Philip says, "Lord, show us the Father and that will be enough!" As I read that verse, I put my name in place of Philip's. I had been calling myself a Christian for over twenty years, but I did not really feel that I knew him, at least, not in the way that he wanted me to know him.

I continued reading that passage, where Jesus continues to teach his disciples by telling them in so many words: "Look, Philip, if you cannot believe me for who I say that I am, then believe me because of the works that you have seen me perform." Then, in verse 12, he says, "Truly, truly, I say to you, he who believes in me, the works that I do shall he do also; and greater works than these shall he do; because I go to the Father." As I read this, it was as though the verse supernaturally jumped off the page and into my spirit. I simply bowed my head and prayed, "Lord, help me believe." In the remainder of that chapter, Jesus teaches his disciples about the Holy Spirit and how he will send the Holy Spirit to those who love him and love his Father. He says in verse 26 that they will not be left as orphans but that when the Helper or Counselor (the Holy Spirit) comes, he will teach them all things and bring all that he has said to their remembrance. These verses and this teaching greatly heightened my interest in the ministry of the Holy Spirit.

Not long after this, while at work, I was examining a patient who told me that one of my cousins was a patient on the second floor. As soon as I had time, I went to see her. She had had an appendectomy the previous day. As we visited, it seemed that every other word she uttered was, "Thank you, Jesus," or, "Praise the Lord." I began to talk to her about my faith walk and my interest in the person and work of the Holy Spirit in the believer's life. She asked me if I had ever received the baptism of the Holy Spirit. She was the second person who had asked me this question. The first had been an X-ray technician at St. Joseph's Hospital. I had responded that I did not know. The technician had replied, "When it happens to you, you will know it."

As I continued my conversation with my cousin, I learned that she was a charismatic Episcopalian. I also met her associate priest when he visited that day. They invited me to attend their home meetings, where they were free to worship without offending anyone. I went. As a "good Baptist," I knew nothing about the gifts of the Spirit. Uncertain about what the meetings would be like, I went with a simple prayer: "Lord, I want to see you exalted as Lord and Savior, and I want to see your love shared among your body of believers." I did not want to be distracted by spiritual gifts with which I was not familiar. I wanted to be open to knowing God more deeply. During the meetings, some prayed or sang in other languages, but they all met to worship the Lord, sing his praises, and grow in his grace and knowledge. I continued attending the meetings, usually going alone while Charlotte remained home with our three children.

Not long afterward, my next-door neighbor Clarence invited me to attend his men's prayer group. He and his wife attended a different Baptist church, which had recently hosted a lay witness mission. It consisted of a series of Friday, Saturday, and Sunday meetings where laypeople, not church staff members, would conduct the services, stay in local church members' homes, and speak about what the Lord was doing in their lives. The men's prayer meeting resulted from that weekend.

I had recently visited Clarence in the hospital before his open-heart surgery. Then, when I attended the men's prayer group, Clarence shared that after I had left the hospital after visiting him, he'd felt a pain across his chest in the shape of a cross. He believed the pain was a sign from God that his surgery would be successful. As we concluded our meeting that night, we stood in a circle, holding hands and praying for the person on our right. When it was my turn to pray, the power and presence of God suddenly filled me from head to toe. The experience was so strong that I was barely able to continue uttering the words of my prayer. I felt like I would surely have fallen to the floor had I not been holding those men's hands. It was not an emotional experience, but rather a very real and powerful spiritual experience.

I believe I was baptized in, or filled with, the Holy Spirit that moment. I left that meeting filled with a wonder and mystery of God. Before then, I had been excited about what the Lord was doing in my life, but after that, I became even more enthusiastic. I left thinking, "Wow, if that is what happens to people as a result of a lay witness mission, then we need to have one in our church." I had recently shared what the Lord was doing in my life with our pastor. I went to him again and asked if we could have a lay witness mission in our church. He asked me if I would lead the mission project, and I eagerly accepted.

Each lay witness mission weekend involved a group of twenty to thirty laypeople who would go into both small and large group settings at a church, sharing stories of what God was doing in their lives. The meetings would begin Friday night and continue until Sunday noon. The laypeople would lead the singing, congregational large group time, and small group break-out times. Friday night small group sessions usually began with the question, "When was God most real in your life?" This would be the primary focus for the weekend. Our hope and prayer were that each person's personal walk with God would be revived, bringing revival for the whole body of believers. Each weekend, without fail, miracles occurred.

The Lord strengthened and renewed many lives during our first lay witness mission. Over the next few years, Charlotte and I became involved in Lay Renewal Ministries and ministered in churches all over South Texas. Almost every weekend became a unique experience as we witnessed the Lord's great works in and through our lives. We saw God work in many lives and many churches during those years. We witnessed many miracles: spiritual healing, emotional healing, and physical healing.

One of the more dramatic experiences happened one weekend when my wife and I were part of the leadership team. Charlotte was helping lead the children's ministry, and I was helping as the song leader. Before departing on Friday, Charlotte and some of the women helping her were having a prayer meeting in our home. Mauria, a member of our team, became acutely ill with rectal hemorrhaging. Charlotte called me at work, asking what to do. Taking my advice, they rushed Mauria to the nearest emergency room at Sharpstown Hospital, where they evaluated and admitted her. I remember praying at work, "Lord, what is your purpose in this, and why has Mauria been stricken?"

When I arrived home later that afternoon, Charlotte met me at the door, saying, "Ralph, we are supposed to go to the hospital and pray for Mauria." I told her we could not go and still make it to our mission destination in Texas City on time. Charlotte did not protest, and we got in the car and headed out. We had to drive about a mile on Bellaire Blvd. to get on the Southwest Freeway, and then we would take Loop 610 to the Galveston Freeway. After only traveling a few blocks on Bellaire, I suddenly experienced a rather sharp pain in my upper-mid abdomen, just below my sternum. The pain did not last very long, so I dismissed it and continued driving. Traveling a few blocks more, the pain recurred, more intense this time and lasting a little longer. I grabbed my upper abdomen and flinched. Charlotte noticed and asked, "What's wrong? Do you have pain in your stomach?"

"Yes," I responded.

She replied, "Well, I told you we were supposed to go pray for Mauria!"

I simply kept quiet and continued driving. We approached the last light on Bellaire before we needed to turn and get on the freeway. Before we could make the turn, I experienced the third episode of acute upper-abdominal pain, this one greater than the previous two.

I glanced at Charlotte and replied, "I think I am supposed to stop by the hospital and pray for Mauria."

When we saw her, she was in considerable pain and distress. I asked where her pain was located, and she pointed to the same location as my three acute episodes. I told her that I was having pain in the same area and that I believed the Lord had sent me to pray for her. I said a simple prayer: "Mauria, be healed in the name of Jesus."

We left the hospital and began driving. However, as we rounded the 610 Loop, I began to experience a warm sensation in my upper abdomen where I had previously had the intense pain. Since we were late to the conference, I was not able to call Mauria to see how she was doing until Saturday afternoon. She said that about thirty minutes after we had prayed for her, the bleeding and pain completely stopped and she was now feeling well again. The hospital discharged her a day later after all the tests came back negative. As it turned out, I had witnessed to Mauria's doctor two years before this regarding the power of Christ to heal today. Mauria was able to tell him that I had prayed for her to be healed. Praise the Lord!

My life was going well. However, my dad's life was not. By now, alcoholism had consumed him. My mom was distraught. She had never so much as tasted a drop of liquor; however, she was living with someone known as the town drunk. Living in a small

DR. RALPH PEIL & DR. SCOTT STRIPLING

town made the addiction impossible to conceal. One day at work, I received a call from our friend and neighbor who had encountered my dad while he was in town to buy a gift for my mom. My dad had drunkenly stumbled to the ground while trying to get in his truck.

When I first found my dad drunk, I tried reasoning with him, but all of my talking only fell on deaf ears. I wanted to follow Scripture's advice and honor my father regardless of whether he was living in a way that was worthy of that honor or not. I realized that I did not have the power to change my dad's life by talking and reasoning with him. I began to trust God and look for ways to honor my dad. Not knowing how else to help, every time I saw him (especially if he was intoxicated), I hugged him and told him I loved him and God loved him.

My mom also did everything she knew to help him. In the morning, before she left the house to teach, she read a devotional from Oral Robert's book *A Daily Guide to Miracles*. However, she never knew how she would find my dad when she returned home. Sometimes he would have a good day and still be sober, but more often than not, she would find him very intoxicated.

My dad had many bad days. An example occurred during quail season one year. Living in the country, we looked forward to hunting season each fall. We often shared opening day of dove, quail, duck, and deer season in the field together. My dad loved to work with and train bird dogs, which we used to hunt quail. A covey of quail exploding from the brush under the point of a good bird dog was always an exciting hunting experience.

My dad was an expert shot and could bring down two or three birds on any given covey rise. However, this particular day, he missed every attempt he made. Frustrated, he left mid-morning. He had clearly begun drinking in the early morning. My friends and I continued hunting. My dad returned about mid-afternoon after having apparently gone home to sober up. Rejoining the hunt, he took down every bird he fired upon.

As we were getting ready to return home that afternoon, a man stopped to talk to my dad. They got into an argument, shouting and hollering at one another. My dad suddenly picked up a shotgun, aimed it at the man, and threatened to pull the trigger. I stood there, appalled that he would even think about doing such a thing. Thankfully, I was able to get the gun away from him and end the ordeal, which shook me to the core. Riding with my dad on the way home, I pleaded with him to get his life back in order. With tears running down his face, he asked me to promise never to tell my mom about what I had witnessed that day. I never told her.

My biggest concern was my dad's spiritual condition. When I questioned my mom, she told me a story. Before they had gotten married, she had been in a revival service that my dad had also been attending. At the end of the service, she had prayed for three young men, one of whom was my dad. At the end of the invitation time, she had looked up, and all three of those young men had gone forward to make a profession of faith.

On May 5th, 1976, Charlotte and I took the kids to my parents' house to celebrate my dad's sixtieth birthday. When I walked into the house, it was dark inside but still light outside. It was evident that my dad was having a bad day, so I gave him a hug and went outside with the kids. After a few minutes, my mom called from the house, asking me to come quickly. Entering, I discovered that my dad had gotten a gun and was now threatening to shoot himself. I eventually convinced him to lie down on the bed, where I calmly reasoned and prayed with him. I pleaded with him to call on the Lord for deliverance. He slowly began to pray, saying, "Our Father, which art in heaven, hallowed be thy name. thy kingdom come, thy will be done on earth as it is in heaven. Give us this day our daily bread and forgive us our trespasses even as we forgive those who trespass against us. And lead us not into temptation..." And then, with added emphasis, he exclaimed, "And deliver me from the evil I feel within!"

When my dad finished this prayer, he got up to leave the room. The prayer was a good start on the road to recovery, but there was still a long way to go. I still felt uneasy. I actually begged him to come home with my family and me, where he could receive our love and support. It was the only time I had ever begged my dad for anything. He refused to leave, saying, "Ralph, I will never leave this place." We went ahead and had his birthday party with the kids, and when we left that evening, both my mom and dad seemed to be in better spirits.

However, the next afternoon, when I returned home from work, I received a call from my mom telling me that my dad was gone. He had taken his own life in the very spot where we had prayed the evening before. As my mom shared this tragic news with me, I had an unusual sense of peace. The Holy Spirit had impressed me with the thought: "Ralph, it's okay. It's okay." I did not understand why or how it could be okay.

We got in the car and rushed to see my mom, whom we found obviously upset and crying. When she regained her composure, I was able to ask her about what had happened after we had left the evening before. She told me that after they'd gone to bed, my dad had suddenly gotten up, knelt down beside the bed, and prayed, "Lord, thank you for this day. It started out so bad but ended so beautiful." Mom said this was the only time she had seen him kneel beside the bed and pray. The next morning, before leaving for school, she'd been reading their daily devotional when my dad had stopped her, taken the book from her, read the devotional, and then led them in prayer. So, Mom had left that day with her hopes raised, thinking that better days were ahead. She'd then come home to discover him dead.

As I have reflected on that day, I have wondered what Mom, my brother, or I could have done differently to prevent my father's suicide. I believe the tempter, the enemy of our soul, the devil, whatever name you may give him, came so strongly against my dad that taking his own life was the only escape he believed he had. I believe that in an act of love, he chose to free himself and his family from the torment plaguing him. I believe I will see my father again in heaven.

For Dad's funeral, our pastor and friend, Jeff, read Romans 8:35–39:

Who shall separate us from the love of Christ? Shall tribulation, or distress, or persecution, or famine, or nakedness, or peril, or sword?

Just as it is written, "For thy sake we are being put to death all day long; we are considered as sheep to be slaughtered." But in all these things, we overwhelmingly conquer through him who loved us. For I am convinced that neither death, nor life, nor angels, nor principalities, nor things present, nor things to come, nor powers nor height, nor depth, nor any other created thing shall be able to separate us from the love of God, which is in Christ Jesus, our Lord.

I hope and pray that each person reading my story will know Christ as their personal Lord and Savior and may experience the indwelling presence of the Holy Spirit. The promise of his Word in John 10:10 proclaims, "The thief comes only to steal and kill and destroy; I came that they might have life and have it abundantly."

6

GOD IS IN CONTROL – SCOTT'S TESTIMONY

THEY TRIUMPHED OVER HIM BY THE BLOOD OF THE Lamb and by the word of their testimony; they did not love their lives so much as to shrink from death. (Revelation 12:11)

Due to my mother's consecration, I do not remember a time in my life when I did not know the basic stories of the Bible. Her parents had come to faith in a tent revival in the late 1940s on Munger Street in Dallas. This is how Munger Street Baptist Church, where my mom was raised, was started. It provides a fascinating glimpse into the revivalism of pre-World War II America, particularly in the South.

After marrying my father, an aspiring preacher, Mom diligently made sure that I was exposed to God and all the means of his grace. My dad, frustrated by his own imperfection, gave up on ministry and pursued fulfillment in various ventures. One of those was moving to the small fishing village of Port Isabel, Texas. A shrimper named Lupe Gonzales rescued my dad and his best friend, Bob Lucas, when they were stranded on a fishing trip at the Mansfield Cut on Padre Island. Dad took this rescue as a sign that he should give up his career in law enforcement as a member of the Dallas County Sheriff's Department, and he entered the shrimping business. Port Isabel was as far south as one could go in Texas, and my dad must have felt that it provided him "elbow room" to pursue his dream of success.

My mom dutifully followed him and made sure that she, along with my older sister and me, attended First Baptist Church of Port Isabel every time that the doors opened – Sunday morning, Sunday evening, Wednesday evening, special revivals, and vacation Bible school. I liked church and, at the tender age of six, found myself pondering my life's purpose and the existence of God. Just before my seventh birthday, I responded to a public invitation by our pastor, Everett Young, to receive Christ as my savior. My mom and sister must have been shocked when I bravely walked to the front of the church. My older sister, Ronette, followed me to the altar. A few weeks later, we were both baptized. My father did not attend.

In the middle of third grade, my dad decided that it was time for us to move back to Dallas. Our family must have been in financial distress, because we lived with my maternal grandmother for about six months before moving back to Farmers Branch, a suburb north of Dallas where we had lived before our South Texas adventure. We eventually settled in a house on Old North street. The happiest time of my young life occurred soon after that when I was in the fourth and fifth grades. My passion was football, but I excelled at every sport. I was even a table tennis prodigy. For a while, my mom worked as a clerk at First Baptist Church in Dallas, where the renowned W.A. Criswell was senior pastor. Eventually, we settled at Valwood Park Baptist Church in Farmers Branch. As was our habit, we attended every time the doors were open.

In 1972, when I was ten years old, The Jesus movement was at its apex. A part of this awakening was a huge movement called

Expo 72. In Dallas, that meant a week-long Billy Graham crusade. Every night, Mom dragged us to Texas Stadium, home of the Dallas Cowboys. While I was restless at the beginning of the week, I was eventually drawn by the Holy Spirit and joined the thousands going forward on the final evening. I wanted to consecrate my life and become a disciple of Jesus Christ, so I walked alone from the top tier down to the same field where my heroes – Roger Staubach and Bob Lilly – played on Sunday afternoons. Coach Tom Landry even shared his testimony one night before Billy Graham preached. Coaches can have a tremendous influence on the lives of young men and women. For six months, Billy Graham sent me a series of Bible studies. I would answer the section questions and mail them back to Dr. Graham. Someone on his staff would grade it and send me the next section. Such was cutting-edge discipleship before the computer revolution.

My parents' marriage was on the rocks, mainly due to my dad's infidelity. Wisely, they never argued in front of my sister and me, so it came as a complete shock to me when my dad informed us that he and my mom were getting a divorce. He took all of the blame, and it was the only time that I remember him crying. My dad had faults, but he was affectionate with his children, and he disciplined us. Both are important. Most importantly, he told me that I was a winner and that I would succeed in life at whatever I put my mind to. I believed him.

Somehow they concocted a plan to save their marriage. We were all moving to New Orleans for a fresh start, so I began sixth grade in an inner-city middle school in New Orleans. It was a major culture shock. It was hard to be a Saints fan, and the school conditions were appalling. They were academically two years behind Valwood Elementary, where I had attended in the suburbs of North Dallas. For a few months, my dad attended church with us, but by the spring, it was clear that the marriage-saving experiment was not working. Dad stayed in New Orleans, and I moved with my mom and sister back to our house on Old North, where I had many friends and was a budding sports star.

I was elated to be back home, but I was angry about the breakup of my family. I resented my parents, and I was mad at God for allowing this mess. Within a few months, Dad remarried a much younger woman, and they had a baby, my sister Lori. Three years later, they had another daughter, my sister Miki. Last year, I had the honor of baptizing Miki, along with her husband, Mando, and my nieces Victoria and Ana Lisa. God can always be relied on to bring good out of suffering and difficulty. Within a year, Mom remarried a much older man. I suppose that Dad was looking for excitement and Mom was looking for stability.

Dealing with divorced parents was bad enough, but dealing with stepparents was worse – much worse. It is hard to be a stepparent, but it is even harder to be a stepkid. Choices had to be made because of my mom's marriage. She was moving with her new husband to Iowa Park, near the Texas and Oklahoma border, and my sister moved with her. My dad had moved back to Farmers Branch. I opted to live with him.

All agreed that I needed discipline and guidance, but both were hard to receive from people that I did not respect. By age twelve, I had begun drinking alcohol and smoking pot. I had also discovered girls, and they had discovered me. I will never forget showing up drunk to baseball practice. My coaches and parents were equally exasperated. I no longer attended church, read my Bible, or prayed. God and I were not on speaking terms.

I was very popular in school and was a star athlete. In eighth grade, I was voted class favorite at Vivian Field Jr. High School, but that did not stop my dad from catching me with an ounce of pot. Looking back, the story is quite humorous, but it certainly was not at the time. Evidently a slow learner, I was expelled from R.L. Turner High School for possession of marijuana the next year. I spent the next two summers earning the credits that I lost. Things were not going well for me.

Neither parent seemed happy in their second attempt at marriage; at least, that was my perspective. Things were especially bad for my mother, whose husband turned out to be a closet alcoholic. Unlike my dad, who usually became affectionate and funny when inebriated, my stepdad (who was six foot three and 250 pounds) became mean and belligerent when "under the influence." On one of my rare visits, he accused me of stealing and decided that I needed a good beating. Even though I was only thirteen or fourteen, I managed to escape. Vengeance became the driving force of my life. I trained vigorously with weights, motivated by the desire to put that monster in the hospital for a long time. Because of this domestic violence, my mom eventually separated from her husband, and she and my sister moved back to Farmers Branch/Carrolton.

At almost the exact same time, my dad decided to move back to Port Isabel, the hometown of his second wife. Instead of moving with them, I moved in with my mom and sister. I slept on the couch and kept my belongings in a closet, but I was happy to be back with my nuclear family. We three had always been very close before the re-marriages.

Money was always tight. I had many odd jobs as a kid, and at fourteen, I lied about my age and was hired as a busboy and dishwasher at the Holiday Inn. Even though I could not get a motorcycle license until I was fifteen, I bought a brand-new Suzuki 100. With a job and transportation, I felt somewhat in control of my own life. My sister and I threw papers for the *Dallas Morning News* during my sophomore year. This meant we were up at four every morning – good training for a future archaeologist, but not an easy task for a teenager. I was voted class favorite at my new high school my sophomore year, but it would be my only year at Newman Smith. In January, my mom informed me that she was reconciling with her husband. This was sickening news to me. My sister and I had to choose to live on our own or with one of our parents – and his or her spouse.

My sister had a job and was allowed to quit school and move in with a girlfriend. My mom and stepdad gave her a good car. Mom deeply regrets choosing her husband over her children. She was focused on following the Bible teachings on submission to her husband and saving her marriage. It was years later when God revealed to her the truth that when remarrying, a parent has a previous blood covenant with his or her children that supersedes the new marriage covenant.

This is a challenge for blended families and, no doubt, is a contributing factor to the higher divorce rate in second marriages. Amazingly, my dad called me and apologized for his past mistakes. He told me that he loved me, which I knew was true, and wanted me to live with him. He promised not to try to control me, which was wise since I was uncontrollable at the time. If he had not taken this approach, I would have likely dropped out of high school and worked full time since I would have chosen to live on the streets of Dallas before ever living with my mom and stepfather.

Finally, Dad told me about the football program in Port Isabel and the beaches of South Padre, just two miles away. The Port Isabel Tarpons had a dominant football program, and I had aspirations of playing college football, so I accepted his offer. In late February of my sophomore year, I moved to Port Isabel for the second time. It was my third high school in three years.

Living in the Rio Grande Valley, where Spanish is as common as English, proved to be another culture shock. I resented this blended culture but, ironically, would later become fluent in Spanish, even preaching in several Latin American countries. I enjoyed living with my two little sisters and am close to them to this day, but my dad's second marriage was not stable. Sadly, problems from a first marriage are all too often carried over into a second marriage. I decided that I could endure the less-than-ideal environment for two years and then I would leave for college. In the meantime, I had sports, beaches, girls, and parties. I worked a variety of jobs, from shrimper to salesman. I trained hard for sports, and I partied a lot.

I had a coach named Eliseo Villarreal, who greatly intrigued me. He had been a two-sport All-American at Sam Houston State University. In one of life's great ironies, he had a roommate for two years named Ralph Peil, the co-author of this book. According to Ralph, he never saw "Chayo" without his Bible. Coach V. was chiseled like a Rodin sculpture, and he always carried a Bible with him. I respected him, and I wanted to earn his respect.

At the beginning of my junior year, he invited me to a Fellowship of Christian Athletes meeting. Even though I had been angry with God for almost five years, I agreed to attend the meeting. As Coach V. talked to his athletes about God and his plan for our lives, my fortifications began to crumble like the walls of Jericho. He challenged us to read the book of Proverbs, find a promise from God, and bring it to the next meeting. I was hooked. I do not remember where I got a Bible, but I started reading it with great enthusiasm. I felt as if the whole Bible was written for me. I found my promise: Proverbs 16:3, "Commit to the Lord whatever you do, and he will establish your plans." Decades later, I was honored to be a pallbearer and to give the eulogy at Coach V.'s funeral, which was attended by thousands of grateful people whose lives he had positively impacted.

Over the next year, I memorized hundreds of verses, and I started going to church again. It felt strange but good when I first walked into First Baptist Church of Port Isabel, where I had been baptized ten years earlier. Brother Young was still the pastor, and many people knew who I was – some from my childhood and others because I was now a star for the mighty Port Isabel Tarpons. It must have seemed strange to see a teenager get up on Sunday morning and go to church by himself. I was learning, like Daniel, to stand alone.

All of this Bible reading and church attendance did not mean that my life had completely changed. I remained trapped in many of my bad habits. My lifelong friend Tim Liberto invited me to move back to Farmers Branch/Carrolton for the summer to live with his family. They were amazing and generous people, and it was good for me to be around a healthy family. I jumped at the chance. Tim and I worked construction, read our Bibles, trained hard, chased girls, and partied. He was starting college in a few months on a baseball scholarship, and I was getting ready for my senior season of high school, hoping for a football scholarship.

In late July, I arrived home from work, showered, and looked at myself in the mirror. For the first time in years, there were tears in my eyes; I had buried my pain deep within me. God's Spirit and his Word had finally broken me. I knelt down next to the toilet and made it my altar. It was not a pretty sight, though it was somewhat appropriate. I surrendered my life to the lordship of Jesus Christ. I found forgiveness for my sins, and I forgave everyone who had sinned against me, including my stepfather. When I stood up and looked at myself again, I was a new person. I had experienced 2 Corinthians 5:17 – all things had become new.

When I returned to my high school, I was a witness for Christ. Although I was a pre-season all-state candidate, I broke my leg in the fourth game of the season. My scholarship offers from Rice and other universities turned into walk-on offers, but that was all fine because God had a different course for my life.

Around this same time, I received a phone call from my stepfather. I grudgingly accepted it. He had quit drinking and had surrendered his life to Christ. He asked me to forgive him for the things that he had done and tried to do to my family and me. He made no excuses and accepted full responsibility. Although, as a Christian, I had already forgiven him, his confession served as the catalyst motivating me to build a relationship with him. It also became less awkward to be around my mother.

Robert and I became close friends, and he was a faithful Christian husband to my mother until his death ten years ago. He was also an excellent grandfather to my niece and my four children. I was privileged to preach the sermon at his funeral. Jesus suffered and died so that we could find forgiveness, restoration, and reconciliation. Only God can make something beautiful out of the ugly things of life.

During my college years, I was very active in campus ministry. In my sophomore year, Janet Zappe, a beautiful young woman attending one of my Bible studies, accepted Christ as her Savior. A year later, she became my wife. We have four awesome children and three grandchildren. Janet has remained by my side for the last thirty-seven years.

Also while attending college, I was baptized in the Holy Spirit, opening the realm of miracles. Typically, life is routine and mundane; however, sometimes God chooses to reveal himself in supernatural ways. Below are a few of the many miracles that I have witnessed. I share these as a reminder that "Jesus Christ is the same yesterday, today, and forever" (Hebrews 13:8).

MIRACLE 1 – SALVATION

It has been a great blessing to lead many people to Jesus Christ and participate in their discipleship. One such example happened in 1981 when I was preaching at Lighthouse Assembly of God in Port Isabel. I had started preaching when I was seventeen, so in 1981, at nineteen, I felt I was an old pro. A mutual friend, Kurt Holland, brought a twenty-five-year-old surfer/drug dealer named Ernie Peacock to church. That night, I preached on the power of the cross. Ernie came under conviction of the Holy Spirit, and at the close of the service, he came forward. Ernie repented (turned away) from his sins and embraced the freedom of the cross. That night, he flushed his drugs down the toilet and never looked back.

I am honored to have also helped Ernie find his wife, Sandra, and to have been a part of their missionary calling. For three decades, this amazing couple has planted churches across Mexico and Spain. Thousands have come to faith through their ministry. We never know the far-reaching impact of our witness for Christ. I still preach the power of the cross and firmly believe that it is the only hope for our broken lives.

MIRACLE 2 – MONEY IN THE MAIL

Twice in the early years of our relationship, Janet and I received money in the mail, which I believe God providentially inspired. The first time was during our engagement. We were really in no financial shape to get married, but I think that my infectious enthusiasm must have swayed Janet. On our way to check the mail, we were discussing how to pay for a wedding.

I honestly believed that God could do anything, and I flippantly commented that if there were a check for a thousand dollars in the mail, we would know that it was God's will that we marry. At that point in my life, I had never even seen a check for that much money. Lo and behold, the first letter that I opened contained a check for a thousand dollars! I was speechless, and so was Janet. We got married on December 18, 1982.

After a few months of marriage, we moved to Guadalajara, Mexico, on a one-year missionary appointment to help our dear friends Franklin and Doris Burns conduct two crusades and plant two churches. We worked tirelessly, usually seven days a week. During the day, we worked construction on the new worship facilities, and at night, we preached the Gospel. Janet and I were on a very tight budget, and one month, we completely ran out of food and money two days before we were expecting our monthly support. I stopped by our postal box, and a woman from our home church had mailed us three one-dollar bills. There was no letter inside, just three one-dollar bills. This seems like very little money today, but then it was enough for us to eat for the next two days. We were learning to live by faith.

MIRACLE 3 – STRANDED ON THE HIGHWAY

Once our four kids were all in school, Janet took a retail sales job. As such, the holidays were a very busy time for her. I was pastoring and teaching part time at the local college, so my time was more flexible. For several years, on Christmas evening, our family custom was to pick up Janet from work and drive from McAllen (near the Texas-Mexico border) to a small farm in Springtown (northwest of Fort Worth) where my mom lived. Essentially, we drove across Texas. This particular year, my mother-in-law was also with us, and we were going to drop her off in Austin. Thankfully, we had a full-size van.

As we were passing through the barren King Ranch, the largest ranch in Texas, I saw a car stranded on the side of the road. As we passed, God impressed me to turn back and help those people. Once my family learned of my plan, they were less than supportive of the idea, to say the least. It was late, cold, and crowded in the van. "These people could be criminals!"

As we pulled up to the stranded vehicle, we recognized two of our closest friends, Isaac and Michelle Hays, youth pastors at our church. They were on their honeymoon, and their car had broken down on the side of the road. This was before cell phones were common. They had been praying for help as we had driven by. My kids adored this young couple and were elated that we could help get their vehicle to a garage in the next town and drive them to San Antonio, their destination. Romans 8:14 says, "As many as are led by the Spirit of God, they are the sons of God." Humorously, my family, who so strongly opposed my rescue plan, all took credit for it after the fact.

MIRACLE 4 – LOST CAR KEYS

One day I was caring for Stacy, a toddler and our only child at the time, before leaving for work. Stacy managed to get hold of my car keys, and when it was time for me to leave, they were missing. Most people can relate to the feeling of panic resulting from lost car keys, especially when there is not a spare set.

I was the associate pastor at a church in Brownsville, Texas, and I also taught English and coached high school football and basketball to support my young family. In fact, I was the head coach and could not be late. After scouring the house without success, I had a moment of clarity. It dawned on me that God knew where my keys were. I knelt and prayed a simple prayer: "Dear God, I know that you know where my car keys are. Would you please reveal their location to me?"

Suddenly, it was clear – I should check inside the hem of the curtains. What? As I moved the curtains, I heard the jingle of metal on metal. I looked inside the small opening, and there they were! As I drove to work, I was overwhelmed, knowing that even today, God still speaks to his children.

Through this experience, God demonstrated his care for the smallest details of our lives. One of my favorite verses is James 4:2, which states, "You do not have because you do not ask." By the way, since that day in Brownsville, I have always hung my keys in a safe and secure spot. Some miracles become unnecessary when we exercise personal responsibility.

MIRACLE 5 – LOST GLASSES

Car keys are not the only things that I have lost over the years. In 2011, I officiated a wedding for my dear friends Tim and Tracy Liberto. The ceremony occurred on a mountaintop near San Angelo in West Texas. The mountain was in the middle of Tim's deer lease, so those who attended the wedding were also able to enjoy some excellent hunting. Such is life in the Lone Star State! My youngest son, David, seventeen at the time, jumped at the chance to join me.

That morning, Tim and I went to the mountain wedding site to create a trail for guests. Using machetes, we cleared the path, tagging it with red tape. The wedding was late that afternoon, and as we hiked the mountain to complete the ceremony, my new boots began giving me blisters. At about the halfway point, something distracted me, and I slipped and fell. Thankfully, I was not hurt and proceeded to conduct the unique ceremony.

Afterward, we hiked back to the bottom. Jumping in Ford F-150s and Gators, we headed back to camp for the celebration. As I hopped in the driver's seat of the truck, I realized that I did not have my glasses. I had my Bible and my blisters, but no glasses. I had just spent four hundred dollars for those transition bifocals. I could function without them, but it meant headaches and no deer hunting. Only David and I remained. I doubted that just he and I could find the glasses, and I certainly did not want to search with my blisters talking to me. I asked David to kindly hike back to the ceremony site in case I had set them down there. I suspected there was little chance of locating them, but I wanted to try.

As David headed back up the rugged trail, I called my mom. I wanted a fellow believer to agree with me in prayer. Mom would rather pray than eat Blue Bell ice cream, so she eagerly prayed with me. Before we prayed, I quoted Matthew 18:19: "If any two of you agree on earth as touching anything that they ask, it will be done by their father in heaven."

An hour later, David appeared on the horizon as the sun was setting. He had not found the glasses on top of the mountain. However, on his way down, he had slipped, apparently at the same spot where I had fallen earlier in the day. He had caught himself with his left hand, which, "coincidentally," had landed one inch from my lost glasses.

Heading back to camp, David and I, along with my mom on the phone, shouted praises to God. In the natural, what had just happened was not possible. Yet sometimes there are holes in heaven, and the supernatural invades the natural.

MIRACLE 6 – PANCHO VILLA NOTE: ALL 400 RESIDENTS CAME TO FAITH ON THE RETURN VISIT.

In the 1990s, I was very active in missionary work in Mexico, especially in the villages high in the Sierra Madre just south of Ciudad Victoria. An elder from our church had made a visit to Francisco Villa, and many people there had come to faith. We eagerly planned a return trip during which all four hundred residents would come to faith in Christ. A four-year drought broke after their initial repentance, so now there was water to baptize the new converts. There was no church in this village, whose inhabitants had killed a preacher who had proclaimed the Gospel to them forty years earlier. I suppose that this should not have been surprising behavior for a village named after the bloodthirsty bandito Pancho Villa. Like the blood of Abel, the blood of this martyr called out to God. Around the year A.D. 200, the Church father Tertullian presciently wrote, "The blood of the martyrs would become the very seed of the church."

Upon arrival, villagers warmly greeted us and led us to a large corral in the center of the village. This would be the venue for our outreach. We cleaned the area and set up our portable sound system. A crowd gathered as we played Spanish worship music. In fact, the entire village showed up. Every man in the village was carrying a gun, and some had multiple weapons. It seemed that the spirit of Pancho Villa resided in these men. The women and children came close to our makeshift stage, but the men all sat on the corral fence in the back.

I preached the power of the cross to liberate fallen men and women from their sins. There was a strong anointing, and many people came under conviction regarding their sins. I addressed the men who were literally sitting on the fence. I challenged them to come forward and exchange their weapons for a new life in Christ. Amazingly, they all came forward and laid down their guns. They prayed to receive Christ as their savior and to start new lives. The women and children all followed their lead. To my knowledge, every soul in that village received salvation that night.

On my next trip there, I saw very few people carrying guns, and we baptized dozens of new believers. Later we built a church facility and arranged for a pastor from Bustamante (ninety minutes away) to hold periodic services there. Like the Methodist circuit riders in colonial America, pastors in rural Mexico often care for flocks in several cities. Seeing this village repent and the men forsake violence in favor of the Kingdom of God was indeed a miracle.

MIRACLE 7 – SHILOH

For several years, I served as the director of excavations at Khirbet el-Maqatir, nine miles north of Jerusalem, in the West Bank of Israel/Palestine. Excavations there revealed the remains from the fifteenth-century B.C. (Late Bronze Age) fortress of Ai mentioned in Joshua 7–8 and what is likely the Early Roman (63 B.C.–135 A.D.) city of Ephraim mentioned in John 11:54. It was a phenomenal experience to lead a team of highly trained and skilled professionals in this historic project.

The Associates for Biblical Research (ABR) excavation started in 1995 under the leadership of the renowned Bryant Wood. I knew we were nearing the end of the project but was uncertain of the exact timing. For about three years, I had been exploring the possibility of a future excavation at ancient Shiloh, the center of Israelite worship for over three hundred years. I sensed that we should do one final season of excavation at Khirbet el-Maqatir and then move to Shiloh in 2017. I shared this with my key staff members and asked them to join me in a time of prayer and fasting. I scheduled meetings in December 2015 with the head of the branch of the Israeli Antiquities Authority, which is in charge of Judea and Samaria. They had recently rejected an excavation proposal from a major Christian university in the U.S., so it was questionable whether they would approve my proposal. I also needed the ABR board of directors to approve my proposal.

I shared all of this with my close friend Scott Windrum, who encouraged me to read 1 Samuel 3:21. Normally, I could turn right to a given passage, but I had left my main Bible at a church in Longview, where I had been preaching the week before. Using my back-up Bible, I ended up in Jeremiah 7. My eyes focused on verse 12, which reads, "Go now to the place in Shiloh where I first made a dwelling for my name and see what I did to it because of the wickedness of my people Israel." While I am an advocate for the systematic exegetical study of Scripture, there was no doubt that the Holy Spirit had guided me to this verse. Go now to the place in Shiloh! My meetings with the IAA and the vote of the ABR board confirmed this. So, in 2016 the excavations at Khirbet el-Maqatir concluded, and in 2017 a new excavation at Shiloh began.

BONUS MIRACLE

One of my earliest memories was of a dream. I must have only been three or four when I first had it. The dream would reoccur every few years throughout my life and would impact me emotionally and spiritually each time that I experienced it. In my dream, I walked alone inside a crumbling fortress. Although I was a child, I saw myself as an adult. I was very interested in the stones and various findings around the site.

Several years into our excavation at Khirbet el-Maqatir, our architect, the renowned Leen Ritmeyer, completed his renderings of what the site would have looked like at the time of the Conquest.

Figure 6.1 – Bronze Age Fortress of Ai (courtesy of Leen Ritmeyer).

I was in shock because what I saw in his drawing was what I had seen in my reoccurring dream. As a result, it is impossible to convince me that I am not doing exactly what God intends for me to do. No adversity in the field has ever fazed me. God truly knows the end from the beginning.

These are just a few of the many miracles that I have witnessed over the past thirty-five years. It is indeed true that "Jesus Christ is the same yesterday, today, and forever" (Hebrews 13:8).

AFTERWORD

The God of the 9:11 verses reveals himself to us in the Scriptures as a covenant-making and covenant-keeping God. He first revealed himself to mankind through His servants in the Old Testament: Noah, Abraham, Isaac, Jacob, Moses, and the prophets. Finally, God spoke through Jesus Christ: "In these last days, has spoken to us in His Son, whom He appointed heir of all things, through whom also He made the world" (Hebrews 1:2). From personal experience, we can affirm that God still changes lives through a saving relationship with his Son, Jesus.

We hope that those who have not yet come to a saving knowledge of Christ will claim him as their Lord and Savior. Repentance from sin and surrender to the lordship of Jesus Christ by faith in his redemptive sacrifice result in the assurance of salvation. The apostle Paul's ministry was to preach the Gospel with power and "to open their eyes so that they may turn from darkness to light and from the dominion of Satan to God, in order that they may receive forgiveness of sins and an inheritance among those who have been sanctified by faith in Jesus" (Acts 26:18). Today, the message of salvation remains an open invitation to each person who places his or her faith in Christ.

Peter's Pentecost sermon in Acts 2 makes clear the way of salvation:

Peter replied, "Repent and be baptized, every one of you, in the name of Jesus Christ for the forgiveness of your sins. And you will receive the gift of the Holy Spirit. The promise is for you and your children and for all who are far off—for all whom the Lord our God will call."

Many believers are not victorious in their walk with Christ because they have not fully surrendered to his lordship (authority and control). All believers are called to be ministers of the Gospel, whether vocationally or personally. However, many Christians feel "they are working for God but not with God." This is a difficult place from which to attempt ministry or to live abundantly in Christ. Many who find themselves in this place ultimately drop out of ministry or the Church altogether. This happens when those who are called to lead and serve focus on the ministry of God instead of the God of ministry. One pastor expressed it this way when he said that he felt his sole responsibility was to "find out what God was doing and to get in on it."

Far too many depend on their own strength and are not relying on the strength and ministry of the Holy Spirit at work in them and through them to accomplish the work of Christ. Jesus promised that he would not leave his disciples as orphans, but that he would send the Helper, the Holy Spirit. God's Spirit enables ministers and laymen alike to know and express him in new and powerful ways. Just as the disciples and apostles in the book of Acts "turned the world upside down," God, by his Spirit, is moving powerfully throughout the world today.[1]

The promises of Christ are as real today as they were in the first century. Many people still live unfulfilled lives as Christians and as ministers of the Gospel because they have not discovered the ministry of the Holy Spirit. It is like "trying to run a car with no gasoline or like trying to operate a flashlight with no batteries."[2] The Holy Spirit is the agent of power for proclaiming the good news of the Gospel, for doing the work of the ministry, and for enabling believers to live victorious in covenant with Christ so that they may enjoy his abundant blessings.

Those who live in covenant with God and each other face times of crisis with great confidence. God allows crises upon the world stage to direct us back to him. Our ancestors faced enormous challenges: Armenian genocide, bubonic plague, the rise of militant Islam, and world wars. COVID-19 will also pass soon from a present crisis to historical event. Our hope is that in this present crisis multitudes will prosper through covenant with God and bring hope to the world.

WORKS CITED

Doyle, Tom, and Greg Webster. *Dreams and Visions: Is Jesus Awakening the Muslim World?* Nashville: Thomas Nelson, 2012.

Finkelstein, Israel, Shlomo Bunimovits, Zvi Lederman, and Baruch Brandl. *Shiloh: The Archaeology of a Biblical Site.* Tel Aviv: Institute of Archaeology of Tel Aviv U, Publications Section, 1993.

Ferguson, Everett. *Church History: the Rise and Growth of the Church in Its Cultural, Intellectual, and Political Context.* Grand Rapids: Zondervan, 2013.

Garrison, V. David. *A Wind in the House of Islam: How God Is Drawing Muslims around the World to Faith in Jesus Christ.* Monument: WIGTake Resources, 2014.

Obama, Barack. *The Audacity of Hope: Thoughts on Reclaiming the American Dream.* New York: Crown, 2006.

Obama, Barack. *Dreams of My Father: A Story of Race and Inheritance.* New York: Crown, 2004.

Otis, George. *Informed Intercession.* Ventura: Renew, 1999.

Roberts, Oral. *Daily Guide to Miracles*. Tulsa: Pinoak Pub., 1975.

Scazzero, Peter. *Emotionally Healthy Spirituality: It's Impossible to Be Spiritually Mature While Remaining Emotionally Immature*. Grand Rapids: Zondervan, 2014.

Sutton, Ray R. *That You May Prosper: Dominion by Covenant*. Tyler: Institute for Christian Economics, 1987.

SUGGESTED READING LIST

Anderson, Neil T. *Released from Bondage*. Nashville: T. Nelson, 1993.

Burpo, Todd, and Lynn Vincent. *Heaven Is for Real: A Little Boy's Astounding Story of His Trip to Heaven and Back*. Nashville: Thomas Nelson, 2010.

Broocks, Rice, and Gary R. Habermas. *Man, Myth, Messiah: Answering History's Greatest Question*. Nashville: W. Publishing Group, 2016.

Conner, Kevin J. and Ken Malmin. *The Covenants: The Key to God's Relationship With Mankind*. Portland: City Bible Publishing, 1997.

Evans, Craig A., and Jeremiah Johnston. *Jesus and the Jihadis: Confronting the Rage of Isis: The Theology Driving the Ideology*. Shippensburg: Destiny Image Publishers, 2015.

Fee, Gordon D., and Douglas Stuart. *How to Read the Bible for All Its Worth*. London: Scripture Union, 1994.

Fee, Gordon D. *How to Read the Bible Book by Book: A Guided Tour*. Grand Rapids: Zondervan, 2009.

Henley, Wallace. *GlobeQuake: Living in the Unshakeable Kingdom While the Whole World Falls Apart*. Nashville: Thomas Nelson, 2012.

Intrater, Asher. *Covenant Relationships: A Handbook for Integrity and Loyalty*. Shippenburg: Destiny Image Publishers, 2016.

Johnston, Jeremiah. *Unanswered*. New Kensington: Whitaker House, 2015.

Lucado, Max. *Come Thirsty*. Nashville, TN: W Pub. Group, 2004.

Shetler, Joanne, and Patricia A. Purvis. *And the Word Came with Power: How God Met & Changed a People Forever*. Portland: Multnomah, 1992.

Strobel, Lee. *The Case for Grace: A Journalist Explores the Evidence of Transformed Lives*. Grand Rapids: Zondervan, 2015.

NOTES

1. COVENANT PERSPECTIVE

1. Marcion was the son of an early Church bishop in a region on the south coast of the Black Sea in what is now Turkey. Everett Ferguson, Church History, 85–88.
2. The platform, still standing, is the size of twenty-two football fields.
3. Luther led the intellectual opposition to the last caliphate, ruled by Suliman the Magnificent, to threaten Western civilization.
4. The ruins of a village from the time of Jesus lie amid the modern Arab village of Hizme. A stone vessel factory operated on the northern scarp in late-Second Temple times.
5. There is no evidence that President Obama ever practiced Islam. On the contrary, it is clear that he embraced the revolutionary branch of Christianity known as liberation theology. His mentor was the radical Reverend Jeremiah Wright. Liberation theology purportedly seeks to overturn existing political and social structures, thereby empowering the lower, disenfranchised classes of a given society.
6. Bartleby worked on Wall Street in New York. This was the very power structure that 9/11 terrorists sought to destroy.
7. The walls, in fact, were Middle Bronze Age in construction; however, this is a separate matter from when they fell.
8. The last-minute codicils to Herod's plan of succession created so much uncertainty that it had to be interpreted and executed in Rome by Augustus.

2. BIBLICAL COVENANTS

1. It is unclear if the flood covered the entire globe or just the world as they knew it. It is possible that other humans survived outside the region where Noah and his family lived. There are over two hundred cultures that have similar flood stories. The best known is the Babylonian version known as *The Gilgamesh Epic*.
2. This date is based on I Kings 9:15, which states that the Exodus occurred in the 480th year before the building of Solomon's temple. There is widespread agreement that Solomon's temple was built in 967 B.C. Thus, 967 + 479 = 1466. This date is confirmed by Judges 11:26, where Jephthah states that Israel had been in the land for three hundred years. Jephthah is clearly dated to c. 1100 B.C. 1100 + 300 = 1400.

3. The Israelites were not able to obey the commandments of God that were given to Moses, nor were they able to consistently adhere to all the rules and regulations that were subsequently given. We have the same problem today, but God has provided Jesus Christ as the mediator of the New Covenant.

4. Finkelstein, Israel, Shlomo Bunimovits, Zvi Lederman, and Baruch Brandl. *Shiloh: The Archaeology of a Biblical Site*. Tel Aviv: Institute of Archaeology of Tel Aviv U, Publications Section, 1993.

5. David's tabernacle foreshadowed the Church. In Acts 15:15–18, James quotes Amos 9:11–12 to make this connection.

6. Huss also prophesied just before his death that in one hundred years, God would raise up a messenger whose voice would not be silenced. A century later, Martin Luther launched the Reformation.

7. At present, we cannot be certain if Jesus died and resurrected in A.D. 30 or A.D. 33, but the weight of evidence favors A.D. 33.

3. SOMEONE CALL 9:11 - PART ONE: THE OLD TESTAMENT

1. The Israelites likely had numerous campsites (Hebrew – "gilgalim"). Archaeologist Adam Zertel identified six footprint-shaped sites which may have been these Israelite campsites.

2. The snake on a pole is a common symbol of healing. The staff of Asclepius (Apollo's son), Greek god of healing and medicine, had a snake wrapped around it. The staff of Hermes (the caduceus), Greek god of communication and travel, had two snakes wrapped around it. Since the Hebrew tradition predated the Greek myths by more than two centuries, it is logical to assume that the Greeks were influenced by the Hebrews. Interestingly, in Jerusalem at the Pool of Bethesda, a site of one of Jesus's healing miracles, the Romans built a temple to Asclepius in the second century.

3. A second Passover was celebrated in Numbers 9, and according to 1 Corinthians 5:7, "Christ our Passover lamb has been sacrificed."

4. This is the same passage of Scripture where it is stated, "For God so loved the world that He gave His only begotten Son, that whoever believes in Him, should not perish, but have eternal life" (John 3:16).

5. Tall el-Hammam is being excavated by Trinity Southwest University under the direction of Dr. Steven Collins. Scott Stripling worked as a supervisor on this project from 2005 to 2010, and Ralph Peil worked as a volunteer in 2008.

6. He then adds a quote from Leviticus 19:18b: "You shall love your neighbor as yourself. There is no other commandment greater than these." Jesus then declares, "On these two commandments depend the whole Law and the Prophets."

4. SOMEONE CALL 9:11 - PART TWO: THE
NEW TESTAMENT

1. Matthew's gospel was primarily written to a Jewish audience, as evidenced
   by more than fifty quotes from the Old Testament and seventy-five allusions
   to Old Testament events.

AFTERWORD

1. NKJV, the Open Bible Expanded Edition. Thomas Nelson, Inc., 1983.
2. Pastor Jim Leggett's sermon at Grace Fellowship (Katy, Texas) from March
   20, 2016.

Made in the USA
Coppell, TX
30 March 2022

75746080R00100